Garuda Purana is one of the most sacred Mahapuranas for the devout Hindus. It gains importance because of a single factor : It is the only Purana which gives a detailed description of the postmortem conditions and rituals as believed by this faith. However, it is a belief as spread by the dogmatic priestly class. The fact is that the Garuda Purana contains many more details other than these. It reveals the consequences of an action in a very graphic and logical way. While most of the puranas tell one what to do, it also tells us what one should not do!

Garuda Purana

Garuda

Purana

Compiled by
B.K. Chaturvedi

DIAMOND BOOKS

ISBN : 81-288-0155-4

© Publisher

Publisher : **Diamond Pocket Books Pvt. Ltd.**
X-30, Okhla Industrial Area, Phase-II
New Delhi-110020
Phone : 011-51611861-865
Fax : 011-51611866
E-mail : sales@diamondpublication.com
Website : www.diamondpocketbooks.com

Edition : 2005

Price : Rs. 75/-

Laser Typeset at : R.S. Printers
Printed by : Adarsh Printers, Shahdara, Delhi-110032

GARUDA PURANA   Rs. 75/-
by B.K. Chaturvedi

Preface

This Purana will answer all your queries related to deliverance and salvation. You will be more informed on the body's emancipation after death.

Since this Purana throws in so much of information in the narration, while containing the narration as in the text, a separate chapter called 'Interlude' has also been sandwiched to make the reference of other non-death relation - details more comprehensible. Copious foot-notes have been given to help the uninitiated learn and appreciate the details in the right perspective. In the end, the 1000 names of Lord Vishnu have also been appended, because it is believed that since this Purana reveals the grim reality of this mortal world in a most uninhibitive manner - that is death - the reader may derive solace by chanting these holy names.

Lastly, the translator-cum-interpretor wants to share his gratitude with Narendra ji of Diamond Books for taking up such a daring project with his readers. May Lord Vishnu shower his grace upon all of us.

—**B.K. Chaturvedi**

Contents

Introduction
To The Garuda Purana

The Garuda Purana has come to the so thickly linked with the post-mortem ceremonies among the Hindus that it has perhaps never been studied as a Purana deserving a separate study. The traditional Hindus must have heard it only in the hours of some personal grief and sorrow. Its association with the post-mortem rituals has been so strong that the general belief is that he who needs it in his normally happy time might suffer some personal sorrow. The traditional and obscurant priestly class has deliberately woven a taboo around it, perhaps for the reason of its individual benefit! In the absence of its getting a chance of being read independently, the priests are likely to say the last word about it. And they have succeeded to a great extent in having this rare Purana projection as some jinxed tome - to be touched and interpreted only by those greedy priests. Thanks to the inquisitive mind of the NRI's younger generation which started questioning the relevance of these rituals which apparently looked absurd to them since they didn't know the rationale behind them. This work tries to explain the relevance and provides a fillip to the apparent illogicality.

Most of the times, it is asked as to why such horrendous details have been given which appear downright reprehensible. Why this vivid description of the hells and why this elaboration on the punishments for different crimes? But when the people raise such questions, they forget one basic fact of human psychology. The whole idea behind this lucid details' description is to raise the fear against committing a wrong and unrighteous act. The recitation of this Purana after a person's death in the traditional Hindu households is recommended only for instilling this fear in the hearts of the listeners, so that even if they are on the wrong track, they may still mend their ways. It is the negative way of leading the persons to the righteous track. Furthermore, the details of the hells and the punishment don't appear to be entirely without a sense of logic. If one usurps another's share in money, in the next birth he is likely to be a pauper himself. This is in fact, what is called the 'poetic justice'. So, even if one may not believe in the certitude of the consequences of a wrong action, the logic inherent in these descriptions may convince the people of treading only the recommended path.

In fact, this is the basic thought behind all these Puranas. Although the word 'Purana' originally means 'ancient' or 'old narrative', long before the beginning of the Christian Era, it designated a class of books dealing among other matters, with old-world stories and legends of India. The purpose of compiling these into the form of the tomes was to make the ancient thinking process, its norms of righteous conduct etc available to the subsequent generation, so that with the past experiences and present observations, the ethos of the people of a particular region could be developed. Through the narration of various anecdotes and legends it is repeatedly hammered on the people's pysche as to what is good and what is bad. The stories, epilogues and the parables in the Puranic texts, were put together, but not for the purpose of furnishing a chronologically accurate history. It should be borne in mind that these were composed to furnish the living examples and models of virtues. Though each Purana exalts a particular deity, it must be noted that the catholicity and the uniformity of the Hindus approach to the Supreme Reality is affirmed at every turn.

One word about why Lord Vishnu chose to reveal these details of the post-mortem rituals or ceremonies to Garuda, his mount who was (and is) not likely to face them as this Great Bird is also said to be immortal. Perhaps, Lord Vishnu chose Garuda because the latter has access to every realm, whether it was a hill or heaven - the sublime Vaikuntha lok, or the dreadful Patal lok. Since Garuda is the source of this Purana, it is generally believed that be might have as well checked all these details himself, before passing them on to the sages from whom Vedavyas received them and compiled them in the form of the books. This way it bears a sort of authenticity from the competent authorities.

Secondly, in their description of the negative human aspects, one can also gauge the extent of human depravity. One may be amazed to learn that though this Purana was compiled millennia ago, it contains every conceivable crime that human beings could commit, right from the most lowly incest to even sodomy.

All told, even though the apparent garb of the myths may look absurd and ludicrous, the essence lying with it is quite enlightening and educative. Since this Purana deals more in 'don'ts' and by inference on 'dos', it forms the moral code for developing the penal system for all classes of people. It reveals the logic of the moral working at the back of this ancient culture. Of course, there may have been very many inter pretations, but they reveal, in the final analysis, the importance attached to these Puranas, which reveal what we have been and what we aspire to be.

1

Departure Of The Soul From The Body

Long, long ago, in the Nemisheranya region, the high sages like Shaunak and others had started a Yagya together, lasting for about a thousand years, so that they could get a berth in heaven. In that region had also come Soota ji, who was quite honourably welcomed by the sages present there. Soota ji was an expert in reciting various mythological tales and he had a long experience. Having welcomed him, the sages asked Soota ji; "Please describe to us about this creation, the gods, the realm of Yama and which good or bad deeds lead a man to get which form in the next life."

Soota ji said: "Narayana Vishnu is the sole doer (Creator) of this creation. He is Narayan, because he dwells in water [Nava = water, ayana = dwelling place]. He is the Lord of Lakshmi. Having repeatedly incarnated Himself to destroy iniquity on the earth and redeemed it from the sinners. It was he who incarnated himself as Rama to redeem the sages and seers from the tyranny inflected on them by king Ravan of lanka. He was incarnated as Lord Narsimha to slay Hiranyakashyapa and redeemed the earth. It is this Lord Supreme Vishnu who is the Primal Creator, Sustainer and its Destroyer in His dreadful Rudra form. In his Vaaha (Boar) incarnation he slayed Hiranyakashyap to redeem the earth. He had also incarnated in the form of the fish. Sage Vedavyas is also born out of his partial grace who authored all the Puranas."

"If Lord Vishnu is the best tree in this world, its root is righteous faith, the Vedas are its branches the various Yagyas are its flowers and the final salvation is its fruit. So, ultimately it is Lord Vishnu who is the final bestower of all reward of all worship and even the final salvation."

[Then recounting a story, Soota ji said]: Once Goddess Parvati asked her spouse Lord Rudra (Shiva) that even when he himself was a supreme Lord of this world, who it was in whose worship he remained ever engrossed. "After all, who is that Lord Supreme whom you worship." "I worship Lord Vishnu

12

the sole Lord of this entire Creation who is also ever revered by various other gods and sages."

The same question when asked by Shaunak and other sages, Soota ji said: "Lord Vishnu is the sole base of this entire universe." This precisely, was the answer that Lord Shiv gave to Parvaii. "It is Lord Vishnu the Lord Supreme who incarnated in various forms, viz, Narsimha, Rama, Krishna etc. to protect the righteous faith on this earth. In the form of Lord Rama, he destroyed the demons; as Lord Krishna he destroyed those with a wicked mentality, as Varah he redeemed the earth and as Narsimha, while protecting his devotee Prahlad's life, he had destroyed Hiranyakashyapa. It is to him that I owe reverence, closing my eyes."

Hearing these details about Lord Vishnu's greatness, bearing the authority from Lord Shiv himself, the assembled sages became all the more curious,. They asked Soota ji: "Sir! Whatever you have told about Lord Vishnu is merely dispeller of all fears. But, tell us about the afflictions and agonies that trouble the being in this realm and the next. Please tell us in detail about the way to the Lord of Death, Yama. What sort of tortures the beings are subjected to in his realm."

Getting the question, Soota ji said: "Well! Now, I will tell you all that I have heard Lord Narayan enlightening Garuda, in this context."

[Then Soota ji starts to narrate]. The way to Yama's realm is highly inaccessible and difficult to explain. Yet, for your knowledge I attempt to describe it.

Once Garuda had asked Lord Vishnu: "O Lord! Even when it is easy to chant your name, still men deprive themselves from it and eventually reach hell. Devotion to you is open through many avenues to be covered with a variety of paces, as your once told me. But, at present what I want to know from you is that what sort of the way the one deprived of our grace has to travel. What problems will they face in traversing that path. Please tell me in detail as to what fate the one deprived of your devotion faces."

Lord Vishnu said: "Garuda! Now, I tell you about the way to Yama as you have asked me. It is by traversing this path that the accrued being reach the realm of Yama. Their description is horrendous. They fall into hell those who are self-conceited, violent and arrogant, due to their wealth and position. They invariably develop demonic tendencies and eventually fall into hell. Those who are infatuated with sensual

13

and mundane pleasures and forget God also fall into hell. But, those who try to redeem themselves by donating alms are spared from this fall. But the sinners and evil doers suffer torture, while going to the realm of Yama. Now, I will describe to you the grip that the sinners suffer in this world and the next, following their death.

"A man enjoys good or bad consequences in accordance with the good and bad deeds that he had committed in the previous life. He suffers some dreadful afflictions, owing the remainder to the effect of his bad deeds committed in the previous life. Agony and the fear of a calamity befalling him keeps him on the tenterhooks. Such a man, even though becoming agony less in his youth and well served by his sons and wife, suddenly confronts death in the form of a snake which bites him to cause his end. Even if he survives upto his death, he passes his old age almost listlessly. He has his hunger waning which, too, remains insatiable by the food that the house-owner may throw before him, as stale food is thrown before the dogs. Soon, that fellow would have his vocal chords obstructed by rampant phlegm in the body. His bones ache and it becomes difficult for him to move about. A wheezing sound is constantly heard in his voice. Due to waning consciousness he remains lying on the bed thinking about his woebegone life. Even though surrounded by his kith and kin death keeps on approaching him. His sensual powers grow very dim and he even fails to respond when accosted. This way, keeping his thoughts concentrated on his family, welfare and not on God, he dies amidst the loud wailing of his family members and friends.

"O Garuda! Exactly as the time of death, a man develops divine vision like the gods. At that time he sees the world thoroughly instinct with Lord Almighty and becomes incapable of speaking. The waning sensual powers turn an animate being also into an inanimate being. It is the time the messengers of death approach him. When the five basic elements depart to these parent sources, the man feels as if a second is passing in a century's time. He suffers the agony as through he is being bitten by a 100 scorpions. When he beholds the messengers of death before him, out of sheer fright he starts oozing saliva and froth from his mouth. Since many sinners have their mouth passage obstructed, their life also escapes from the body through the anus-way. At the time, life escapes from the body, he sees the messenger of death :

redenned eyes with anger, huge and weird mouth, carrying a staff and a noose in their hands. They gnash this teeth and are always unclad. Their hair stand on end, they have their horrible mouth, with nails as big and sharp as though they carry an incisive weapon. Seeing such dreadful messengers, the dying man often passes stool and urine out of sheer fear. He cries in pain, but the messengers wrists a thumb-size subtle body from the dying man's physique. But that subtle form keeps on gazing at its original form. Putting a noose round that subtle form and tightening it, they carry it away, as though a king's soldiers are dragging away a criminal. Even while dragging it along, the messengers of death often threaten that subtle form of the dead person, further frightening his that form with the eerie hell that lies ahead for him. These messengers say: "O wicked soul ! Move fast as you have to go to Yama-loka (Yama's realm). You have to stay in the dreadful hell like Kumbhee pāka and others. So, you do not delay." Hearing these harsh words of the death messengers and the waiting cries of his near and dear, that being (the dying man) cries in uncontrollable pain. The messengers subject the subtle form to a variety of tortures and agonies. The messengers' constant threat breaks his morale as well. Sundering with pain and fear, that being moves along. He feels very thirsty and hungry, but he has to pass in the scorching heat and walk over roasting sands. He doesn't get any shadow at all, not allowed to rest even for a second. But the messengers of death keep on whipping it mercilessly. He moves, falling repeatedly on the way. He faints and loses his consciousness, but move he must. This way he is taken to Yama's realm in about a couple of Muhurtas. (a small unit of time).

"Reaching the death realm, be remains there for a little period, he returns to the men's realm, after getting permission from Yamaraja. As he reaches the mortal world, he tries to re enter his old body. But noosed by the messengers, he doesn't succeed. Then due to unbearable hunger and thirst he cries and keeps on suffering the agony. His allowed diet is only the Pindas and libation[1] offered by his sons, but remains thoroughly insatiated. On the contrary, a little food offered

---

1. It is a sort of food dedicated to the body of the dead persons, according to the Hindu belief generally it is made of the cooked rice. The believed objective is that the Pindas provide strength to that subtle form to reach upto Yama's realm.

this way further whets his appetite all the more. The libations offered hardly quench his thirst. Those beings who don't receive post morten food in the form of Pindas and libations this way remain loitering in an eerie jungle, hungry and thirsty. Unless the after death ceremonies are duly performed, the soul remains hungry and thirsty for even a eons.

"O Garuda [says Lord Vishnu] that Pinda is divided into four parts. Two of them are meant for the consumption of the five basic elements which provides strength to the subtle form. The third part is given to the death messengers and the fourth part is given to that person's ghostly identity. This way the Preta (ghostly form) of that person gets the Pinda for nine days. On the 10th day the Pinda-daan creates the full body of the ghost which makes it movables. O Best of the Birds! Even when that person's body is destroyed through incineration into subtle form, it gets a physical entity by the Pindas. It is with that little form it has to suffer the consequences of its good and bad deeds committed in his life on the earth.

"Now I describe how that subtle body is created by consuming the Pindas. The Pinda of the first day forms the head of the subtle body, of second day the its neck and shoulder, of the third day, its heart. The Pinda of the fourth day forms the back, of the fifth day the navel; of the sixth day the waist, anus, the organ and other limbs. The Pinda of the seventh day forms the bone and that of the eight and the ninth day, thighs and feet. It is on the tenth day that the offering of the Pinda generates hunger and thirst in that body. So formed out of these pindas the sublte body becomes capable of partaking the food offered in the Shraddha on the 11th and 12th day of the death of that person. On the 13th day, tied in the noose of the death messengers like a monkey tied in ropes held by its trainer, the being comes to this world in isolation.

"O Garuda! Taking out the dimensions of the river Vaiterani, the realm of Yama spreads to 86000 Yojanas. Now this subtle form of that (dead) person has to traverse the path at the rate of 247 Yojan[1] in every 24 hours, in the company of those messengers of Death. He has to pass through 16 halts or settlements on the way. They are : Somyapura, Shaumipura, Nagendra Bhavan, Gandharva, Shailagan, Kraunch, Knoorapura, Vichitra Bhavan, Dukkha; Nama Knandapura,

---

1.   Nearly 8 miles by the earthly units.

Sutapta-Bhawan, Raudra Nagar, Yoyovarshana, Sheetadaya and Behubheeta. Beyond these, lie Yamapura. This way tied in the Yama's noose, leaving all his kith and kin and his place, that sinner's soul traverses the path to Yama's realm.

While moving on this way, the being has to suffer untold agonies, but he doesn't get any relief. All the time, he broods over his (mis) deeds and suffers grief. But surprisingly, having inferred such pains and agonies, when he gets his next life, he again forgets God and indulges in bad deeds and evil actions.

2

The Vaiterani River

Learning briefly about the realm of Yama from Lord Narayanan, Garuda said: "O Lord! Really the way to Yama's realm is so frightening and full of grief? Please also enlighten me as to how a sinner-being is drawn to that realm. How is he or she taken to that way?"

Lord Narayan replied: "The way is really frightening even by learning about that. Even though you are my staunch devotee, you may shudder to know about it. In that Yama realm there are no trees to provide any redeeming shades. No kind of food is available there to let the being get some strength to face the daunting troubles. Neither is available even a drop of water. The being that has to pass through it remains hungry and thirsty always.

"O Lord of Birds! In that realm all the twelve forms of the Sun burn as brightly and scorchingly as they do when the Final Dissolution (Pralaya) period commences. The atmosphere is extremely inclement there. There, the being is made to get stung by poisonous huge snakes, pierced with the most incisive thorns and is often thrown before the wild and hungry beasts. Now, the poisonous deadly scorpions are fed on the being and now that sinner is burnt in the blazing fire. After this halt, there is a two thousand Yojan spread wilderness, having many sharp edged leaves called the Asipatra vana (a jungle teeming with leaves, having as sharp leaves as the edge of a sword). That Jungle is replete with frighteningly huge crows, vultures, owls and the deadly bees. When bitten by all these vultures and insects, the being reaches beneath a tree and the sharp edged leaves inflict deadly wounds on his subtle body. In that jungle only, there are many eerie blind wells in which he is made to fall into. He is also tossed down from the high mountains. Repeatedly, he is made to walk on the path littered with sharp nails and thorns. Frequently, he is thrown inside the weird caves, thrust deep into dirty grime filled ponds and often leeches are let loose on him. Now, he is made to walk on the boiling sands and now thrown over the live ambers. He is also taken through suffocating smoke-filled chambers. Sometimes, he is also made to stay in a pit filled with pus and blood. Mid way he also comes across a river called Vaitaraṇi which is extremely frightening even to look at. This river is 100 Yojan broad, filled with pus and blood and its embankments are made with bones. It is very deep and very few are able to go across. it has thick deadly algae and abound with ferocious gladiators. The meat-eating birds, especially, remain all around it. The sinners often fail to go across it.

"O Garuda! As the clarified butter boils when heated by fire, so this river's fluids boil on seeing an approaching sinner. The insects with sharp tongues remain ever ready to prey on the approaching sinners. When the being is cosigned to this river, he often cries bitterly remembering his kith and kin. This river has only pus and blood to quench the thirst and decomposed flesh to satiate the hunger. Falling into the vortex of the eddies, the being often goes down and comes up. Not even for a moment can he remain at rest.

"O Garuda! This river has been wrought only for torturing the sinners. It is so huge and wide that nobody can see its other bank. This way, crying and wailing, yelling for succour, the sinner crosses this river and reaches the Yama loka. The tortures inflicted in this realm are too repugnant to even describe. Now, the messengers of death drag the being, tying him up with this noose, whose ropes pass through the subtle body's nostrils or the ear holes. With their hands and feet tied, the sinners are made to carry a huge weight. When they fail, the messengers of death beat them with iron clubs. As a result, often the siners move, puking blood and writhing in pain. Still, those ignorant do not remember God, but weep in the memory of their kith and kin. At times, they repent quietly: "We came into this human species after doing much meritorious deeds in our earlier lives. But in the last life neither did we do any righteous deed, nor donate alms to the needy, nor worshipped Gods. Neither did we take a dip in the holy Ganga, nor serviced the holy men. Neither we had any sweet-water ponds made for the birds' benefit, nor did we feed the pious Brahmans. Now my soul! you cannot escape these deadly consequences. Never did we listen to the recitation of the noble Puranas, nor ever revered the learned Priests. Neither did we obey our masters, nor discharged filial responsibilities. (The female sinner thinks) Neither did I remain faithful to my husband, nor even served him devotedly. Neither did I committ myself to Satihood at the pyre of my dead husband. It was because of my previous lives' unrighteous deeds that I got this body of a woman in my last life. But even then I failed to do anything to improve my status in the species-echelons."

This way all the sinners-whether male or female-keep on wailing and repenting on their mistakes and lapses while being dragged along on this torturous path.

Further, Lord Narayan told Garuda: "The ghostly (Preta) form of the dead person survives for 17 days in an eternal form. On the 18th day, it reaches the town called Somyapura, which is replete with ferocious ghosts. In this town exists a beautiful banyan tree, with a river called Pushpabhadra close by. For sometime, the being rests here with the accompanying death—Messengers and keeps on grieving, remembering his relations. But he (or she) is accosted by the death messengers: "To where have vanished all your relations now? Here, nobody comes to your rescue, save your own good deeds. Now suffering the consequence of whatever you have done in your previous life, keep moving on the path shown by us." They also threaten the being with their own might. You cannot get away from us. Unfortunately you did nothing in your life to escape your treading this horrible path. [i.e. you accumulated no good deeds to escape these troubles]. Now it is your destiny to keep on moving on this path. You fool! Why did you never listen to anybody to take recitation by a noble Brahman. Did you ever realise that in Yama's realm you will have to beg for everything. This knowledge is known to even an ordinary child. Now you suffer for your mistake." This way, taunting the being the death-messengers keep on beating the subtle form with iron clubs. The being has no option but to faint in agony and wake up in extreme anguish. Even when he trues to run away, he is heavily beaten to make him fall in the way. Again, he has to get up and tread that torturous, inescapable path. That being is taken on this path on the 13th day of his death and after 17 days of his departure, he reaches Somyapura. There, he gets the first meal offered by the Shraddha performed by his sons (after the first month of the death). Then he is taken to Saunipur, where a regent of Yama remains in position. That is the second halting place.

After this, following the three fortnightly period, the being partakes of the cereals and libations offered again in his Shraddha by his descendants. Then, crossing this halt, the being reaches Nagendra Bhawan where he again feels melancholic seeing an eerie forest and weeps. It is this place where he raves and rants when the messenger of death drag and pull him along. It takes two months', time for him to cross this jungle. Then, the being partakes of the food of the Shraddha performed by his descendants after two months, of his demise. Then, he is again taken along by the death messengers. In three months, after death the being in the subtle ghostly form reaches the place called Pattanpur and receives the food offered by his family members. In the four months', period, he reaches the place called Shailpur where he is constantly stoned by the messengers. Following this, he gets the food offered by his family members[1] from which he derives some solace. Then he reaches Knonchapura where he receives the food offered in the fifth month and subsequently, he is taken to a place called Krookapura. When he reaches here five months and fifteen days get elapsed to his death in the mortal world. Here, he stops for a while. Then he is again tortured by the messengers of death and they drag him along further ahead to reach the place called Chitra-Bhawan. This place is ruled by Yamaraj's younger brother called Vichitra who has a very dreadful physique and looks very eerie. The being feels very much frightened seeing him. He wants to get away, but he is forced to remain there. Then, he reaches the river Vaiterani where many boat-men stand to take him across the river. They tell the being: "If you have any merit to your credit you can go across. Else we won't take you across." In fact only that being can go across this river who has donated a cow. Those who haven't done so remain wistfully looking at the other bank. Meanwhile, the messengers of death keep on showing the boiling, dreadful, river. and try to make him go into it but he keeps on crying. He who has donated a cow in his life is able to go across it when thrown into it. He who has not done so drowns in that weird river. The messengers go across through the aerial way and they get a hook entangled into that being's mouth, with whose help he goes across. Reaching across the being who had donated a cow gets the food offered in the Shraddha by his descendants after six months of his death. But by this time due to extreme exertion, he remains hungry and keeps on crying, insatiated. The messengers of death take the being to the place called

1. Following the 13th day of the death ceremony on every Amavasya (moonless day) the being is offered food by his descendants.

Bahvapada, reaching there he gets the food offered in the seventh mouth of his Shraddha. This intake gives him some satisfaction.

Further, Lord Vishnu tells Garuda that the being is taken to the place called Duphadapur: Moving through the aerial route, he encounters many kinds of afflictions and receives the food offered in the eighth month of his Shraddha. At the completions, of the 9th month, he reaches Krandapur. He beholds many Krandaganas (groups that rave and cry) and seeing them, he also cries. Here, he is again tortured. In the 10th month he is taken to Supta-Bhawan-pur where he receives he 10th month's Pinda. From here, he goes to the Randra Nagar to receive the Shraddha offering on the 11th month of his death. Having partaken of the food and drinks, he reaches Paryovershana Nagar after the 15th day of leaving Randrapur. This place is a very frightening place when on the being keeps pouring the clouds raining grief. At this place in a short time he gets a very little of the Shraddha offerings. At the completion of one year of his death, the ghostly form of the being reaches Sheetadya Nagar. This place is even colder than the Himalayas. The being shudders in unbearable cold. He madly pines for a support, but he gets nothing. He longs for some of his kith and kin, but the messengers tease him: "What merit have you accrued to your name to desire some succour here." You did no noble work to receive any rescue at this place. Severely tortured, internally, the being helplessly moves forward and feels somewhat satisfied to receive the offerings made in the Shraddha on the completion of his death of one full year.

After this, he is taken to Bahubheetapura where he sheds even his subtle form, no bigger than a thumb.

This way the meritorious work that one accomplishes in his mortal life gives the being solace in this dreadful journey. These who haven't are subjected to untold tortures and miseries.

Lord Vishnu Said. "Garuda ! This is the description of the way that leads to Yama's realm from the southern gate of it. Now you have known how a being after his death completes one year on the way to Yama's realm and how he is tortured and tormented. Now what else do you desire to listen further from me?"

3

The Tortures Suffered

Upon the Lord, asking thus, Garuda ji submitted: "When the being reaches this way to Yama's realm, what kinds of tortures does he have to suffer."

The Lord said: "Now I describe the full details of this hell hearing about which even my devotes shudder in fright and so shall you two."

The Lord said: "O Garuda! Beyond Bahubheetapura there lies the huge realm of Yamaraja, spread for about 44 Yojanas. Reaching there, the being cries loudly. Hearing about the fresh arrival Yamaraj instructs the sentinels of the realm called Dharmadhwaja who ever dwells there. Dharmadhwaja then reveals the being's record before Chitragupta. O Garuda! Yama knows very well about the atheists ever indulging in evil deeds. But he confirms about the same from Chitragupta who, despite being well-informed asks about the being from Shravan, capable of roaming about every realm at will and a son of Brahma. Shravan has special prowess in knowing, seeing and listening about the things that aspire even quite far from him. He has many wives who also enjoy this facility. These women know well about their jobs. These shravan family members know all about a being's manifest and even unmanifest feelings and sentiments, besides all their actions and thoughts. They pour out every detail about the being before Chitragupta. He then tells everything he knows about a being truthfully. Those beings-men-who are able to propitiate him by their noble actions like donating alms and keeping strict vows go to heaven or they even receive salvation of their soul in certain cases. Shravan also tells about the diehard sinners and criminals. Like the sun, the moon, fire, sky, land, water etc. which are the agencies to learn the real truth about a being, Shravan and Yamaraj, in fact, through their access, ever remain stationed in a being's heart. So having ascertained all the facts about a being, Yamraj summons a sinner being who beholds Yamaraj's frightening form: a huge body like the dark clouds, raining rains of dissolution, adorned in lighting, flash-like garments and having 32 arms. His body spreads to 3 Yojanas, his eyes like a small well; eerie, ferocious teeth; red eyes and a long nose. His lieutenants are Kaal (Time), Jwara (fever) Vyadhi (diseases) and including Chitragupta, all have grisly figures. They roar loudly to make the being frightened and cry in fright. He now repents not having donated alms and doing some noble deeds. On the instruction of Yama Chitra pronounces his judgement saying: "O Sinner! Why have you accumulated so much sin in arrogance? Why did you indulge in wrath, lust etc. and pile up so much sin. Now, enjoy the suffering the same way that you had enjoyed your pleasures. Don't be sad now for you are reaping what you have sown. Now no concession to possible. Our Lord Yama is totally impartial in his justice to every being, no matter whether he is a scholar or dunce, rich or poor, strong or meek." Hearing these words, the sinner (being) requests about his past and keeps quiet. Then Yama (Dharma) gives his final verdict: "go to hell you ruthless sinner!" Yama's assistants named Durdanda, Prechanda, Chanda etc. tie that being in their noose to drag him hellwards.

In hell exists a huge tree like the blazing fine, spreading to five Yojana in breadth and one Yogan in height. Tying the being against one branch of this horrendous tree, the messengers beat the being. Bound to that fire-raging tree, the being cries but gets no relief. That cotton like inflammable tree has many sinners hanging with their heads down. They all supplicate before the messengers: "Forgive our sins." But, unmindful of the supplications the messengers keep on beating them with clubs and spears, iron staffs and maces. The sinners often faint at which the messengers accost them sarcastically: "Hey sinner! Why did you commit such vile acts. Why didn't you give water to the thirsty, food to the hungry? They were not difficult jobs, were they? Even half a morsel of food you never offered to a dog or a crow. Neither you ever welcomed your guests duly nor offered oblations to the departed souls? In order to escape yourself from the torture did you ever think about Yamaraja or Chitragupta? Did you ever chant the holy mantras? Neither did you visit the holy spots, nor worshipped the deities. Even while remaining in the family, you never offered cereal as alms. Hence you are undergoing these tortures. Since you never cared or did servie to the holy saints, you have to suffer its consequences. You have to pass the sentences pronounced by Yama. Remember that Hari (Vishnu) is the Ultimate God who can pardon your sin now. We punish only at his command."

Saying so, they beat the being who falls from that fiery-tree as if he is a live ember. Even while falling, their physical consciousness gets wounded by the sharp-edges leaves of that tree. Their physical hits falling below are lapped up by the beastly dogs. This makes the being cry all the more. But throwing dust in the being's (or beings) open mouth after tying him (or them) in the ropes, the messengers keep beating the being with the clubs. Some of the sinners are torn apart from the middle as a pieces of wood is sewn. Some of the sinners are made to lie on the ground and then they are hacked to pieces. Some of them have their lower half of the body pushed into the ground and the upper half is targeted with keen arrows. Some are crushed into the crusher. Some are fercibly made to sit on the live embers. Some are boiled in the boiling oil. Some of them are thrown before the mad pachyderms and some are dropped from the heights. All of the sinners are made to fall prey before the incisive beaked grisly birds. Even amongst the sinners, feuds continue. Some demand from the other the loan they had given to them in the mortal world. The messengers settle their accounts by saving pieces of the bodies of the debtors. This way after punishing them, the messengers consign them to many sections of the hall like the Andhatamaisra and others where the sinners are further tortured and tormented. Perhaps the most cruel punishment is that which is meted out to the sinners under that fiery tree. That cannot be fully described even.

O Garuda! There are 8400000 sections of hell. Among these, the ones that give the most excruciating punishment are 21 : Mahararava, Taamisra, Lohashanku, Kummal, Shalmabi, Raurava. Kaalsootraka, Lohitda, Pootinimitaka, Sanghat, Savisha, Sampratapen, Mahaviraya, Kakola, Airchi, Sanjivan, Mahapath, Andhatamisra, Kumbheepaak, Samprataan, Ekatapana. These sections of hell give a variety of punishments to the sinners. All of these are duly guarded by the messengers of death. Lying consigned to these hells the sinners, iniquitous persons remain there for many years. In these hells, the pairs (man-woman) have to pass the sentence together. Here, the distinction is made between those that had observed their filial duties and those that had not. Since their Nemises catches with them, they have to pass their full sentence as decided by Yamaraj. It is only after suffering the consequences of their misdeeds or sins that the beings (their soul) are allowed to take rebirth on the earth. This way, this Yama loka and its punishments are very horrendous. But one cannot escape going there if one has accumulated sins to one's name.

4

The Sins

Garuda again asked: "Lord which are sins that cause the being to pass to this huge realm of Yama and which make them fall and drown in the river Vaitarani? Which are the sins that push the being into hell? Please explain in details."

Lord Narayan (Vishnu) said: "Those who are even engaged in the vile and inauspicious engagement keep on going from one section of the hell to the other. However, those whose conduct is righteous come into the Yama's realm though its gates on the east, west and north directions. It is only the sinners and the wicked who come into it from the southern gate. Now I tell you in details. The river that inflicts great torture on the wicked beings flows south of Yama's realm. The wicked get into the realm in accordance with the intensity of their sins."

Enlightening Garuda further the Lord told him that those that kill a Brahman or a cow or a child; who hit a woman, that cause abortion and commit heinous sins clandestinely get drowned in the river. Those that steal Guru's and the divine property, usurp a woman's property, eat up a child's share keep on coming to Yama's realm day in and day out. Those that take the loan but don't repay, indulge in a betrayal, treat people to food mixed with poison, adopt to other's vices, feel jealous against those that are virtuous; move in bad company and avoid the noble one; the calumniators of the sacred texts, the guru, the Brahmans and the gods; who detest holy places; that take delight at other's distress, that speak harsh words, that don't pay regard to the learned scholars, that deem themselves to be erudite scholars, without themselves, knowing anything also keep coming to Yama's realm through that-southern - gate only.

Those who drown in the Vaiterani are those that insult their parents and elders; that desert a devoted wife; that cast aspersions on the noble and holy Sadhus; that don't donate alms to the Brahmans with a firm resolve; that destroy the Yagyas; that usurp the land meant for grazing the cows fall

26

into the river Vaiterani. That Brahmans who sell jaggery, sugar, honey, sweets, ghee, milk or salt fall into that river. The Brahman husband of the woman of loose morals, the Brahmana slayer of the animals other than prescribed for sacrifices in the Yagya, the Brahmans who deviate from their ordained duties and partake of non-vegetarian food, the Brahman who drinks wine, who is of cruel nature, devoid of the scriptural knowledge go into that Vaiterni. The Shrodra that reads the Vedas and drinks the milk of the cow Kapila, that marries a Brahmana woman; that who wears the sacred thread, who elopes with other's woman, who desires copulation with the king's wife, who deflowers young girds, who deceives honest, devoted and cultured women get drowned in the river. In short, all those who waver from their scripture - ordained path get downed in the river. Even when they cross the river to reach Yama's realm, on the Lord Yama's instructions, the messengers of death again bring them back to the river to drown them in that river.

Telling further about the 22 sections of hell that were recounted earlier, the Lord said: "O Garuda! Among all the sections these 21 are the deadliest. Those who have not donated a black cow are cosigned to those trees that grow on the bank of the river Vaitarani. Those that give false evidence; practice a false faith, amass wealth through deceitful means; destroy gardens and parks, earn their bread through foul means, cut high trees; shun visiting the holy teerthas; rape a widow and those woman that think of other men - are hanged front that fiery (cotton-like) tree and subsequently put into the various hells in a most cruel fashion.

They suffer untold tortures who are atheist, who violate traditions; who torture their own dependents; who remain engrossed in worldly pleasures; who dupe others by their vain glorious pretenses and who are ungrateful are consigned to deadly sections of hell. Those women, sons and servants who deprive their masters of their food also go to these hells. Those who eat without offering the share to the deities, and the Lord of sacrifices, Vaishwadeva certainly go to hell. Those that obstruct the public passage with thorns, barbed wires or stones etc. also go to hell. Those ignorant who do not serve their gurus or deities like Lord Shiv, Vishnu, Sun, Ganesh, and the Goddess like Parvati surely deserve to go to hell. The Brahman who forgets about his duties and sleeps with a maid goes to hell. That Brahman who produces his progeny through

27

the womb of a lowly maid also goes to hell. Such a Brahman is a rogue and he doesn't deserve any respect. Those men who remain indifferent to the gods also go to hell. Those who do not disengage the two fighting cows or Brahmans, but even provoke them to fight more surely go to hell. If the husband doesn't remain close to his devoted wife in her 'Ritu-kaal' (when she wants to indulge in the copulation most) he surely goes to hell. Those in their blinding lust copulate with a woman passing through her menstrual period, those who copulate with women, even in water and on the day of the Shradda go to hell for sure. Those who put their stool or urine inside fire and who pass stool or urine in a garden or the place where cows remain go to hell for sure.

Those who don't follow the dictates of their religion, who manufacture swords and other weapon cannot escape hell. A trader selling skins, woman selling her body and a person who sells poison also cannot escape hell. Those who don't pity the hapless and shelterless, who carry grudges against the noble, who punish someone for no fault go to hell. Those who don't offer food to a hungry Brahmana, begging for food even though the food is ready in their kitchen cannot escape hell. Those who for the love of their pleasure don't observe the due rites also go to hell. Those who don't call the one Guru who imparts them the spiritual knowledge; don't consider him to be the Guru who recites to them the holy Puranas also go to hell. Traitors of friends, the unfaithful persons in love, the ones who deliberately belie an innocents' hope surely go to hell. Those who ruin marriages, trouble the pilgrims are consigned to hell permanently. Those who set fire on the settlements are caught by the messengers of Yama and dropped into the blazing fire pots. When they cry for coolness on getting burnt, the messengers take them to the jungle, teeming with sword-like sharp edged leaves. Their burnt bodies get easily cut by those leaves. Then the Yama- messengers say sarcastically: "O sinner! Now have your cool sleep!" When that being demands water, the messengers offer him boiling oil and force it down to that being's, mouth which incinerates his intestines. This way such beings are constantly tortured by the hench persons of Yama.

Lord Vishnu said to Garuda: "I have given you only a brief account of these hells and the sins that take the beings to them. This way suffering most horrible miseries till the Pralaya. Then they get reborn only in the new age. But the bodies they receive is the same which they had before the Pralaya. Some of the beings with Yama's permission get birth as the trees and other inanimate objects. Trees, hushes, creepers, mounts, leaves, grass, flowers etc. come in this category called Sthavar. But there are 84 lakh species of the animate beings. It is passing through these sub-human species that the fortunate ones get born as humans. But those that get rebirth here as humans comming direct from the hell become Chandal (Pariahs) etc and those humans that are afflicted with a deadly disease like leprosy etc.

Man must realise that there is no escape from the consequences of one's actions. Hence man should shun evil deeds.

5

The Righteous Norms of Living

Upon being asked by the sages as to how a being could get out of the clutches of the consequences of his evil deeds, Shaunak ji said: "O sages! Hearing this Garuda Purana, one realises one's bounded duties. In order to fulfil one's mission, it is essential to court company with the nobles and shun that of the wicked persons. Real brother is he who cares for your and other's interest. He who has a religious bent is the real good associate. He who has his wealth destroyed may go to the teerthas (holy places). He who loses his allegiances to truth and righteous duty has no place to go exept hell. The drunkards, back-biters, those who appear as false witness remain for long sunken in the river Vaiterani. As has been told, those that break into other houses; destroy public property, those who recklessly womanise; those that indulge in vile acts also remain sunken in that river in the most horrible conditions. It is by avoiding these acts that one may escape going to hell. But in no way one's vile deeds consequences can stop visiting upon one. Perhaps a change in heart by worshipping God may bring some redemption in these conditions."

Hearing this the sages asked: "O Soota ji! Please enlighten us as to which God should be worshipped." Who is the creator and sustainer of this whole creation? How that Supreme Lord can be propitiated? Who are his incarnations and how their dynasties continue? Please tell us in details."

Upon this Shaunak ji recounted the conversation that took place between Brahma ji and Vyas ji. Brahma ji was asked by Vyas ji: "O Lord why this most blessed Purana, the Garuda Purana, was revealed by Lord Hari (Vishnu) to Shiv and other gods?"

Then Brahma ji said: "Once I happened to visit Kailash mount in the company of some other Gods. There we had the Darshan for Lord Rudra (Shiv). We saw him lost in meditation. We asked him: "O Lord, who is that who commands such devotion even from you as well."

Answering my question, he replied: "I was concentrating my thoughts on the supreme God Lord Vishnu - the bestower of every revered, the omnipresent and omniscient Lord. O Pitamaha! (Grandfather)! Even I who keep my body smeared with ash and grow long tendril locks also worship him only. He is the ultimate refuge of everyone. The whole creation is ever instnict with only his presence. He is beyond the distraction of truth and untruth. He is the ultimate object of every being - whither animate or inanimate - worship. He who has Agni (fire) as his mouth, the sun and the moon as his eyes, the sky as his navel, the feet this earth and the divine realm his head. I ever worship him only!"

Then Shaunake ji dwelt upon the various names of Lord Hari: he is Vasudeva because he looks after everybody's prosperity; Vishnu because he ensures every being's salvation if attempted through the night course; Hari because the whole world at the time of Dissolution gets usurped or stolen by Him only. Those that worship him with this knowledge have their desires always fulfilled.

Then diverting upon the various noble acts and the righteous conduct, Shamnak ji said: "One should never stay where there may not be a king, a physician, a river and a learned Brahmana. One gets the reward of one's action without fail. The merit accrued to one due to good deeds profound in the past lives show their effect only at the ordained time. External conditions might aid or abate a result, but they cannot cause it because its cause is only one's action. Like a heifer gets to its mother - cow, no matter if there are billions of cows, the same way the consequences of one's action gets to the doer of the act."

Further he said: "O Brahmans!' One should try to stay in this world like a lotus in the flower. Because if one remains attached to the worldly pleasures, one may not get away from their allurement. The real bliss dwells only where there is aversion to wordly attachments or Nrivitti. It is attachments which breed sorrow at their non-fulfillment which in turn gives rise to anger to pollute one's mind. So one should stay indifferently in the world while constantly keeping one's attention riveted to Lord Vishnu.

Enlightening the sages further, Soota ji said: "In this world one has no real friend or foe. It is due to one's vested interest that such emotions emerge. Nevertheless, one should keep on fulfilling one's mundane obligations. For nobody is sure as to what lies in store for one self. One should not wonder if a loquacious person is recognised as an erudite scholar and a beautiful woman is honoured for her piety. Very rare is a poor not indulging in vile deeds and a moneyed man not thinking of his next birth. Of course, most of the person appear what they are actually not, but even one transparent personality may glorify the whole community like a single son may bring laurels to an entire family."

Further continuing on the worldly conduct, Soota ji said. "One should pay full attention to one's son till he becomes five years of age. After this the boy gets some idea of what is really good and bad for him. But between 6 to 15 years treat your son with constant reprimand in order to prevent him from going wayward. But as soon as he turns 16, start treating him as your friend.

"When one loses one's father, his ideal guardian almost like his father - is the elder brother. After father's death to an elder brother, the younger one is like his son and to the younger brother, the elder brother is like his father. If the brothers remain united, nobody can trouble them."

"There are four kinds of people who are by nature rogues. One who is ungrateful, the after who is non-Aryan, the third who carries a grudge for a long period and the fourth who has a wicked heart. One should even avoid their company.

"One gets position in the society by one's deeds and not by one's popularity. A lion is not duly appointed a jungle's king; it becomes the ruler merely by its strength and power. A lazy trader, a pleasure-loving servant, a moneyless teacher and a foul speaking wench never succeed in their mission."

"Separation from one's spouse, disgrace among one's own kith and kin, an unrepaid debt, a compulsion to serve a wicked person, indifference of friends due to one's falling in evil days burn one's heart very severely."

"The five situations that can redeem oneself from the very causes of sorrow are: seeking noble company; having a skill to earn money; having an obedient and loving wife; and knowing the regimen to keep the diseases at bay."

"The deer, the elephant, the fire-fly, the bee and the fish suffer doom because of their infatuation to the perception of one's sense. While the deer gets trapped by listening to good music that through its ears; the elephant by being touched by something titillating; the fire-fly by beholding the burning fire; the bee by tasting the pollen of the flower and the fish by smelling something enchanting. Each of these beings die because of their one sense; uncontrollable infatuation. But man goes to his doom by his infatuation to his each sensual perception. Hence he carries the five causes of his death always on his body."

"Never let even an iota of any of the following afflictions remain: the diseases, the fire or the debt. Even a birth of them can aggravate to cause the doom."

Concluding his discourse, Soota ji said: "Righteous conduct and the discretionary wisdom always help one to lead life successfully and happily. They should never be ignored."

6

The Consequences of the Sins

Garuda asked: "Lord ! What are the tale telling Symptoms of the sinner. How can we identify as to which sinner has committed which sin."

The Lord replied: "One gets afflicted by tuberculosis when one kills a Brahmana. The slayer of a cow becomes humped-back. The slayer of a girl becomes a leper. In the next life, they are born into the community of Pariah (Chandala). He who destroys the embryo and hits a woman gets birth in the Mlechcha community. He who copulates with his Guru's wife becomes afflicted with a terrible skin disease. Those Brahmanas who eat everything recklessly become pot-bellied. He who doesn't offer food to others that is their due becomes afflicted with goitre. White leprosy afflicts those that perform the Shraddha with impious food. He who insults his guru becomes afflicted with epilepsy. The caluminator of the scriptures suffer from jaundice. One-eyed, and blind become generally those that ruin a nuptial union. A liar generally becomes a stammerer. A thief of gems in the earlier life gets born into a lowly family. He who steals herbs and vegetables in this life gets birth as a peacock in the next life. He who steals cotton is born as a sheep. An arrogant person gets birth as an elephant. The Brahmanas who eat food from low caste people's hand get birth as a leopard in the next life. Boar becomes that Brahmana in the next life who conducts Yagya everyone for the low-caste people. The hypocrites get the birth of a heron. Vultures' species is of those Brahmanas who duped others in their priestly duties. Those who force their invitation on others are born as a crow in their next life.

The Brahmana who imparts knowledge to the undeserving becomes a bull in his next life. The disciple who doesn't serve his mentor will get birth as a beast. Jackal becomes that Brahmana who backs out on his word. The one who condemns caste-system become a pigeon, a duper an owl and the traitor of a friend a hilly kite. He who steals other's woman, betrays friends become the red patridge. The daughter in law who

34

abuses her mother-in-law becomes a leech in the next life. She who insults her husband becomes un ugly bird. An unfaithful wife becomes a she-snake. Those who marry in the family become bears in the next life. A king raping a minor girl becomes a python. He who has an illicit relation with his friend's wife becomes a donkey. A sodomist becomes a pig in the next life. A leacher in this life becomes a horse in the next. A wine - addict becomes a wolf. A thief of gold get born as an insect. He who usurps other's wealth becomes a deadly ghost."

"O Garuda! [says Lord Vishnu] Those who steal a Brahman's property have their family destroyed. "An evil doer suffers badly in the present life and then suffers the tortures of hell after his death. It is only when his demerits are exhausted by various tortures that he becomes deserving to get rebirth as a man. In the intervening time, he keeps on getting birth in the sub-human species."

Now Garuda asked the Lord: "How a being gets existence in the womb and what kind of troubles he suffers in that position."

The Lord replied : "The first day after her menses, the woman is called Chandali, the second day Brahma-hatyari (A killer of a Brahmana) and the third day she is called a 'Rajaki'. Conception on these days lead to the birth of the sinners. So in the three days immediately after the menses, the woman should not be copulated with."

"On the first night (after the conception) the embryo is called 'Kalala' after five nights, a 'bud-bud' and after 10 nights, it becomes a piece of flesh. Its head is formed after two months, after three months nail, skin bristles, bone, skin and the organ start coming into existence. After four months, all the basic elements show their presence in the embryo. In the fifth month, it starts feeling hunger and thirst. In the sixth month, it gets covered by a pellicle. Covered with it, the embryo also starts moving in the right sides of her mother's womb. It has to remain covered with its own refuses and has to suffer various sensations caused by his mother's eating hitter, sour or astringent food items. It is writhing in that agony that it starts to pray to god for its early exit. As the 10th month comes, it becomes prepared to come out to the world. Labour pains in the mother are caused at the Lord's inkling. The prayer said by the child inside the womb destroys all his previous lives 'Immures." Then describing these tortures further, Lord Vishnu satisfied the Garuda's curiosity. While dilating upon the importance of having a son, Lord said: "A son ensures his father's redemption from the hell called 'Pu'. In fact a noble son rectifies all the mistakes of his entire family members. One who happens to behold one's grandson's face has his berth assured in the heaven. But one's progeny must continue through only legal wedlock. Only a legally produced or adopted son ensures this status to his sire or grandsire. In this context I recite to you a story."

"Once there was a very righteous and noble king in the Treta Age called Valair Vaahan. One day he went for hunting and shot down a deer which far off, even though wounded. Chasing it, the king happened to reach a very eerie jungle. He espied a water-pond and took a bath in it along with his horse. Then, as he was about to relax under the shadow of a huge tree, he suddenly found a grisly figure confronting him. Upon inquiry that figure revealed that it was a 'Preta' (a ghost). He had to remain in this form because he had no friend, son or kith who could perform his last rites ritually. Since he had not been fed properly through various post- mortem offering, he had to remain in this form. Even though he might espy fruits he couldn't eat; espy water he couldn't drink only because of this lapse.' The king then promised to complete all the rituals as his king as well. The king had a small gold idol of Lord Vishnu made of '32 masa gold' and having consecrated it, arranged a pitcher through a ritual worship to offer libation to that Preta. With the king taking these measures, the Preta was released from that evil form and got to his due realm."

Hearing this tale and the importance of the post-mortem rituals, Garuda was curious to know about these rituals in details about those person who were very righteous and truthful in their mortal life.

Lord explained : "A righteous one always tries to atone for any evil deed committed by him as death approaches him. At the final hour, they should chant Lord Vishnu's name and offer worship through fruits, sweets and other auspicious objects from his death-bed. The following instructions must be observed when a noble person senses the approach of his death.

(a) Offer food to noble Brahmanas with the Dakshin.

(b) Chant the eight syllable mantra : OM Vishnuve Niamah

(c) Chant the twelve syllable mantra : OM Namo Bhagwate Vasudevay!"

(d) efore remembering Lord Vishnu, concentrates on Lord Shiv's form.

(e) Remember all the ten incarnations of Lord Vishnu (Matsya, Koorma, Varaha, Narsimha, Rama, Krishna, Vaman, Parashuram, Buddha[1] and Kalki)

Chanting of Vishnu's name dissolves crores of afflictions. Ajamila was a rogue, but at the end he yelled for 'Narayan' which was actually his son's name. But since this is an epithet of Lord Vishnu, Ajamila was saved by Vishnu's messengers from going to hell only because he chanted 'Narayana.'

"But he who atones for his sins, but doesn't remember Vishnu's name doesn't get final redemption. If at the final hour, the person's son helps in making the donation, the effect of this act gets accentuated a thousand times. A noble and obedient son must make his father donate alms at the latter's final hour. Alms should include Til, iron, cotton, gold, salt, seven cereals, cow and a piece of land. Cow's donation is particularly important as this ensures the being's crossing the dreadful river Vaiterani without much trouble. Preferably, a red or black cow should be chosen for donation. After its formal worship, it should be given to the deserving person who may tend it well."

In fact, these things donated help a great deal in the soul's journey to the Yama's realm and even in the dead person's next life." Concluding his narration, Lord Vishnu said:

"O Garuda! He who keeps the deities happy by regular donations lives and his life in conformity with the sacred instructions escapes the tortures of hell. Such a man enjoys great bliss on the contrary. Any close relations developed between or among the various persons through birth could be defined as meeting of the various boats that float upon this sea of mortal existence. If they meet affectionately and honestly they have their merit enhanced in the records of Yamaraja."

---

1. Apparently this Purana was compiled after Buddha's advent.

7

The Ghosts

Garuda said to Lord Narayan : "Lord ! Now please tell me as to how they who fall in the category of ghosts could be redeemed from that stage. Please also enlighten me about the various forms of the ghosts and their characteristic features."

Whereupon the Lord said : "Now I tell you about the various identification marks and forms of the ghosts. Their physical appearance seems like made of the wind and hence it is not easily decipherable. Afflicted with hunger or thirst, they reach near their kith and kin and enter their house. At times, their visage appears quite deformed. Although all men dream, some of them find in their dreams tied in chains and feel hungry. They are normally distressed by the ghosts."

"He who dreams travelling astride a bull and experiences as though he is being tossed up into the sky or dreams himself (or herself) dying amidst his (or her) relations gets troubled by the ghosts. When one dreams such dreams and beholds the animals going out of the house, one should realise that his or her being is possessed by some ghostly spirit."

"O Garuda! When someone well versed in the holy Vedas offer libation for that spirit, it gets release from its ghostly form. Remember those ghosts that are unsatisfied - hungry, thirsty or desiring the fulfilment of any wish trouble their close relation. When astrally satisfied, they cease troubling their kith and kin. On the contrary, when such ghosts are released from their eerie form, they even provide additional benefits and help to their relations (in the mortal life). Those beings who having realised the affliction that the ghost is suffering from don't do anything to release him suffer the deadly consequences. Some times even after getting released from his accursed form the ghost suffers deprivation. Such ghosts have their bad deeds vile affect dissipated in the Yama's realm." Whereupon Garuda asked the Lord as to what one should do to get relief from the ghosts. The Lord advised him that the best way to get the desired relief was constantly chanting the Gayatri mantra .

"This mantra is the veritable God in effect and its chanting protects one's interests."

Garuda: "Lord ! How one falls in the form of the ghostly existence."

"Garuda" replied the Lord, " The consequence of one's evil deeds lead him to this form. Those that destroy a beautiful public place - park, temple or an eating joint- often suffer this form due to their vile deeds. Those that cut a verdant tree or a jungle teeming with verdant trees suffer this form. They not only become ghosts but are born in the next birth as a Pariah (Chandal). Those who are killed by the dacoits or thieves also get this ghostly form. In this context I narrate you one incident."

"Dharma raja Yuddhisthar had once asked his grandfather, Bheeshma as to the consequence of which deed make the soul adopt to a ghostly form. And how that soul is released from that accrued existence."

Replying to the questions, Bheeshma said: "In this context I tell you a historical event. In older times there was a Brahmana called Santapta. He dwelt in the forest, in order to complete his penance. He was very pious, learned and righteous, but he was always in the dread of suffering the wretched existence when he would go to yama's realm. He was a noble man, but he had this fear in his heart for some unknown reason."

"This way elapsed many years. Then one day that Brahmana Santapta thought : 'Why shouldn't I visit various holy Teerthas. So he went on a pilgrimage. One day, following his bowing to the rising sun after having his bath in the holy river, he espied five deadly ghosts looking at him. Although he was visibly frightened, yet gathering his courage he asked them: "The consequence of which vile deed made you suffer this horrible form's existence?"

The ghosts replied: "Yes! It is the consequence of our vile deeds and demeanour in our mortal life. We always hated others. With the result, we even remain hungry and thirsty. We have become so dim - sighted that we cannot even recognise the directions. We are totally at a loss to know as to where we should go. We have nobody to guide us."

Then giving the details of their vile acts and their names, the first one said: "Since I always fed the Brahmanas on the stale and rotten food, in this form my name is Paaryushit." The second said : "I always deceived others, so I am named Soochimukha". The third ghost said : "I would always get away seeing a hungry Brahmana at my gate, so I am named Sheegrahak." The fourth said : "I am named Rohak because I would always usurp and eat the best edibles at my relations' house." The fifth one said: "I am named Lekhaka because whenever anyone demanded anything from me, I would start writing on the earth."

Then they further said: "It is due to these vile acts that we got this most horrible, accursed forms. But curiously enough, as we beheld you, we got back our consciousness. Now you can ask us anything that you desire."

The Brahmana Santapta asked: "What is your food. Because food is necessary to survive in any existence." They replied: "We subsist on the edibles consigned to flames through a havana and on phlegm and excreta. We take food where we find filthy conditions. We get food from those houses where there is no piety; where people don't read the Vedas and where no holy Yagyas are performed. Where there is no decorum or propriety maintained, we ghosts get our filling from those houses. Greed, anger infatuation, fear, sorrow are the emotions that make us sustain in this form. Where people are possessed by these vices, we get our food from those houses. Even the most filthy inedible object could be our food. But now having seen you, we are growing averse to all these vile infatuations. Now tell us, what should we do to get out of this ghostly existence."

The Brahmana then advised him: "He who observes holy fasts and vratas never fall into the ghostly existence. He who performs the Yagyas, makes inns and wells for the benefit of the wayfarers; who contribute to have nubile virgins married and who helps people get educated never fall in this ghostly form. But the calumniators of the Vedas, Brahmanas and the cow, the usurpers of other's property, the traitors, the slayer of a cow, the one who copulates with his guru's wife invariably fall in this form."

Bheeshma ji said: "While this conversation was going on, suddenly the flowers were showered from the skies and those 'Pretas' (ghosts) were released from their deadly existence." [The moral of the story is that even the ghosts could be released from their deadly forms, if they happen to get a noble company.]

Garuda, then, asked: "Why do even the noble die untimely. Why the human life span remains so less in Kaliyuga."

Lord Narayan said: "Man lives for his ordained years on the mortal plane. But he can always enhance or curtail his

40

stay on the mortal plane by his noble and evil deeds. He who doesn't follow the ordained path of the community or category one is born in, has his life substantially curtailed.

"Nevertheless, it must be realised that he who is born in this mortal world must die one day- no matter if he is a king or a pauper, a scholar or a dunce."

Then Garuda ji enquired about the post-mortem rituals of the being who expires in his or her childhood.

The Lord said: "If a child dies even before his tonsure ceremony could be performed, his body should be buried and in all post-mortem ceremonies only milk-based libations should be made. However, if the tonsure ceremony of the deceased has been completed before his death, for his soul's satisfaction, other boys of his age should be fed on food and milk. If the deceased dies at five years of age, its formal funeral ceremony should be performed. Remember that in all these ceremonies a 'Ghat' (earthen pitcher duly consecrated) must be donated to a Brahman with a little gold kept in it, in case the donation of pitcher made of gold is an impossible proposition. This satisfies Yamaraj and the deceased is not thrown in the ghostly existence."

8

The Righteous Conduct

Garuda asked : "How can a person attain good sojourn of its soul in heaven? What should a person do while dying so that he may get it."

Replying, the Lord said: "When a man realises that his end is close, he should have a piece of land bemalth or close by a basil (Tulsi) plant which should be duly claimed with a thin layer of cow dung paste spread over it. Then a piece of Shaligram stone should be placed alongside. If one dies even in the shade of Basil, one gets assured of one's salvation. He who dies with a leaf of Tulsi inside his mouth attains access to my (Vishnu's) realm, even though he may be son-less. So, on that piece of land, 'til' grains should also be spread, which should be covered by a thin sheet of a mattress made of the Kusha grass. Kusha, fire, Brahmana and cow never get defiled even when touched by something profane and filthy. On the contrary, that object or person's profanity gets substantially reduced."

"It is on that piece of land the drying person should be asked to lie down or he be placed there. The relations should ensure that the person does not die lying on his cot because it remains above the earth and hence is easily accessible by the messengers of death. When the person has been placed on the consecrated piece of land, a little piece of gold or gem should be put into his mouth. Then a little of Gangajal should be dropped into his mouth. This pious water burns one's sins as quickly as fire burns the pieces of cotton. If possible, the dying person may be asked to utter Ganga's name also. Listening to the pious 'Srimadbhagwata' at this time is also salvation granting. At the time of dying nothing should be given to that person to eat. If that person is still conscious, he may be encouraged to grow totally averse to the world. The devotional songs and discourses at this hour can help the dying person breathe his last comfortably. The nobles make an exit from their mortal coil through the escape gate from the opening of the eyes, ears, nose and throats. The really

42

realised ones (Yogi etc.) also have the life breath finally escaping through their body by splitting a tiny opening at the head or through the crevice made in the palate."

"O Lord of Birds". As soon as life escapes from the body it collapses like a felled tree. Owing to the absence of the vital air, the body starts decomposing soon. So why take any pride on having this fey body?"

"The fire elements then get assimilated back into their parent sources."

Then Garuda asked : "Please tell me also about the dead body's cremation by fire. Also, tell me how and what should the faithful wife do at this hour."

The Lord said "He who doesn't get 'Pinda-dan' (bells of rice made typically for this occasion, donated in the dying person's name) from his son or grandsons doesn't get released from the 'Pitni-rine' (the debt to the ancestors[1]). Immediately after his father's death the son should arrange for the cremation, overcoming his sorrow. He and all the close relations should get all their facial bristles and hair shaved clean. The one who has to perform this ceremony must take a bath before having his hair shaved as also after it. Wearing a white sheet or wrapping with its pieces his private and other parts, he should fetch fresh water to bathe his father's body. Then apply a little sandalwood paste on it and cover it with flowers. First, Pinda-dan has got to be performed. While doing so the five identifying points of the dead should be uttered: his name, his father's, his great great grandfather's, the native place's and of the country's. Then all family members should touch the feet of the deceesed or bless him as the case may be and circumambulate around the body. Now the heir apparent son should lift the body with other's help. The son who carries his father's body reverentially to the cremation ground gets the merit equivalent to performing an Ashwamedha Yagya. He should take a halt in between and offer the second pinda at this time. This makes the Yashas of the ghostly world surround the body for its protection.

"Taking the body to the crematorium the son should place it with its face facing north. Then the ground should be cleaned and smeared with the holy cow dung. Now sprinkling the

---

1. This is one of the three debts that a person must clear before his death. This is paid by helping to continue the limeage. The other two are : Gunu-Rine and the Deva-Rine)

pious water, he should establish the holy fire while saying the prayer : "O God! You are the cause of the world and the repository of all the five basic elements. So, let this deceased person's soul mount to heaven." Having said his prayers the son should lay the pyre made from the woods of Tulsi Palash tree, Pipal tree, while placing a Pinda on the dead man's hand. The son should make sure that he has already made five pinda-dan. Else, the ghostly spirits can disturb the ceremony. Having done so under the instruction of the Mahabrahmana (the funeral priest) the son should set fire to the pyre.

However, those who die during the 'Panchaka' (an inauspicious five days period) don't get good state. Hence no cremation should be performed during this period, normally. But in case it is necessary, then along with the decresed person five effigies charged with the holy mantras should also be burnt.

"In case the wife of the deceased husband wants to become a 'Sati' and get incinerated at her husband's pyre, first she must take a bath. Then decorating herself like a bride, with the priest's permission, bow to the Sun Lord, cirambulate round the pyre and sit on it, as though she is riding her nuptial bed. She who ends her life this way doesn't have her soul suffering any discomfiture. With her body she also has all her sins incinerated. Her soul like the gold in the fire emerges with more piety and merit. Such a woman also dissipates all the sins of her husband and remains in heaventill the reign of 14 Indras. A 'Sati' purifies her entire lineage of all blemishes and enjoys bliss for as many years are there are bristles on the human body. Then with the divine sanction of a long age she is born in a high dynasty of noble virtues and gets the same husband again in her mortal life. The widow who cannot tolerate fire on her body for a little duration burns in the fire of separation for ever. However, she can only cammit herself as Sati when she gets permission from her elders and the priests."

"O Garuda! Then the son doing the ceremony should break the head of the burning body with a wood. The son should convert the humming ceremony into a 'haven'; he should pour over the body Ghee and pray to the fire-god : "Please let the flames burn brightly to consume my father's physical remnants." Thus saying, he should pour in the material till the fire consumes the entire body. A part of the middle of the body is kept unburnt and the same is offered to tortoise and crocodiles. "Having completed it, he should loudly pronounce the name of his dead father while recounting the deceased qualities feeling fully."

"That day the son should not eat. The place the deceased body was kept should again be claimed and for 12 days (nights) an earthen lamp should be allowed to burn non-stop every night."

"The earthen pitcher dedicated to the deceased person-filled with pure water-should be kept at the base of some Pipal tree, either at the crematoruim or some desolate crossing. For three days, water and milk should be poured into that pitcher to satisfy symbolically the thirst of the deceased with the prayer: "May you feel satiated with this libation."

"On the fourth day (after three nights) the remains of the deceased should be collected from the place that the body was burnt. Then the remains should be ritually flown into the pure flowing water. The period the deceased's bone-bits remain in the holy Ganga is also the period his soul enjoys in the heaven."

"In case the deceased's news is received by his kith and kin and not the body (when he has died in a foreign strand), an effigy of him should be made and all the funeral rituals should be done as though the body is present."

"If a pregnant lady dies, her womb should be torn apart to take out the dead child. The child should be burned while the lady's cremation is completed formally like the normal way. In case the boy may have been given the sacred thread, ceremony for his funeral should be completed normally while donating also a sacred thread (Janevo) with the pindas."

"O Garuda!" said Lord Vishnu : "This is how the cremation of the dead should be performed. The spiritually realised person doesn't aid any ritual and they should be (their dead body) should be consigned to a holy river. However, their Shraddha could be performed by anybody having gratitude and faith for them."

9

The Dashgaatra and Other Ceremonies

Garuda, then, desired to know about the ritual called 'Dashagaatra[1]' and who should perform it in the absence of the son of the departed soul.

The Lord said : "Completing this ritual, the son gets redeemed of the debt he owes to his father or manes. The son should complete it with noble conduct, though sorrowing for his father, but not shedding tears for tears cannot bring back the dead to life again. He who is born must die in this world. Had it been possible, the great king like Lord Ram would not have sorrowed for his father. All these relations are temporary like the momentary halt of the travellers going in different ways.

"In case the son is not available, the son's wife (daughter-in-law) can do it. In case she also is not available, the deceased's real brother can do it. This ritual for the ascetic Brahmana should be complied by his disciple. In case no one else is available, the son of the deceased's any brother could do it for his uncle. However, such a ceremony may not remain unobserved and no one be available than the community members, one committee should do it. Doing this ceremony even for the unknown brings the reward equal to one's performing a crore of holy yagyas. In case no one else is be available, the father of the deceased should do it for his son.

"On this occasion only one meal should be taken in the entire day. The day should be spent where the performer should remain spiritually pious and concentrate on the supreme Being.

Right from the 'Dashgaatra' day till the annual day of the death next year, if the son sleeps on the earth taking just one meal for the entire year, he gets the merit of visiting all the holy 'teerthas.' While observing the Shraddha ceremony for

---

1. Literally ten parts of the body. This ceremony symbolically create the vital links of the dead to provide it an entity to reach upto the next realm.

the departed being, the son should worship the Brahmana, drawing his figure on the grass of Kusha. Thereafter, he should proclaim his gotra (lineage) and do the Pinda-daan ceremony. These Pindas should be made of rice or the flour of barley. The sun should request the divinities to let these donated objects reach upto his father (the departed being). Following this, he should have a bath again out of his house and imagine that the subtle form the 'Dashagaatra' (of the departed father) return home (having been claimed of the death ceremony's affliction) keeping his mother ahead of him. Then with a ritual prayer the son should throw away the rice grains-the remainder of the Pindas-wishing prosperity to the entire family of the departed being"

"O Garuda! On that 10th day the final 'Pinda' should be made of the 'Urad-daal' and after the family members have shaven off their head, the Brahmana should be fed on a full feast. He who observes Dashagaatra ceremony of his father has most of the sins atoned for. He gets success and prosperity without any obstruction."

10

The Ekadashah and The Sootaka

Garuda ji asked: "O Lord! Now enlighten me on the Ceremony called 'Ekadashah Rishotsanga.' [The donation of a blemishless bull on the 11th day of the death].

Lord Narayan said. "On the 11th day of the death, early in the morning the son should go to a river or pond and perform the 'Pinda-Kriya': Inviting the Brahmanas reposing faith in the Vedas, he should request them to pray for the liberation of his father's soul from the preta (the evil, ethereal or ghostly) form. Since due to impiety, the Pinda-daan during the first ten days was made without chanting the Vedic Mantra, now on the 11the day it should be done with loudly chanting the same. Then, small icons of Vishnu (gold), Brahma (silver), Rudra (copper) and Yamaraja (iron) should be made. Place them on a clean spot and anoint them with the Ganga jal. Then, the ritual worship of all the gods should be made under the instructions of the priest and the due libation should be made for the departed soul. Then, 11 Brahmans should be fed and the chief priest should be offered all the used personal belongings of the departed person. This should be followed by the donation of a sturdy and blemishless bull[1]. Those of the Brahmana category should donate a yellow bull, while the Kashatriya red-coloured, the traders brown and the Shoodras a black-coloured bull. The bull represents the tangible form of the Dharma. The son should, while donating the bull should pray to it to help his ancestors attain the supreme state.

"If one be convinced that he may never get a son, one may do all these ceremonies himself for his own sake. A married woman dying with her husband and son (sons) be hale and hearty does not require this donations of bull. For her a milch cow should be donated. It must be remembered that the bull donated in this ceremony should not be used in any other work. Else the receiver of it would be commiting a sin."

---

1. This ceremony is called Vrishot sanga or donating a bull. The related story is given in the 'Interlude' section.

"On the occasion of performing the 16 'Shraddha' in the subsequent years, 16 separate 'Pinda-daan' should be made."

"In case a person dies of the fire-burns, these ceremonies should be observed without any change. However, those who die of snake-bite, apart the Shraddha on every 5th lunar day of the two fortnights that the snake-God 'Sheshanaag' should be worshipped. This should be done the following way."

"Make a form of snake with the flour and dough and then with its due worship, all the incense etc. should be burnt around it and eventually, this should be given to the priest with money according to one's capacity. Should one's financial positions be so, one can donate even a small snake-form made of gold. While doing so the son should pray to the snake deity: "O Naag-God! Be propitiated. This should be followed by the 'Navayana Bali-Kriya' under the guidance of the priest and in total conformity with one's family traditions. He who observes these rituals with devotions and faith not only ensures that his father or ancestor gets a good state after death, but his own sins also get duly atoned for. But these rituals are to be observed only after the 10th day when one gets redeemed from the impiety caused by death which is also called' 'Mritak-Sootak.' Having cleaned oneself thoroughly, the 11th day ceremony should be gone through which involves donation of the bed and other personal belongings of the deceased etc.

11

The Sampeedan Ceremony

Garuda then asked the Lord: "O lord! Now enlighten me on the 'Sampeedan Vidhi and the Sootak' while revealing the significance of donating the bed and other personal belongings of the dead person."

Whereupon, Lord Narayan said: "O Best among the Birds! These ceremonies redeem the dead person from that 'Preta-form' and then he goes to dwell among the released ancestors. The son who doesn't conduct the Sampeedan ritual remains impious and under the shadow of the Sootak. Hence this ritual must be observed without fail. It is done in the following way."

"A Brahman after 10 days, a Kshatriya after 12 days, a trader (Vaishya) after 15 days and a Shoodra after a month gets redeemed from the Sootaka. It is believed that the 'Sootak' afflicts the fourth generation for ten nights, the fifth generation for six nights, the sixth generation for four nights and the seventh for three nights. Normally, the Sootak afflicts upto the 10th generation, but for one gotra persons for 7 generations. If someone from the family dies abroad and the news is received after some days, the Sootak period lasts for the family members in accordance with the category as detailed above."

"If a child dies even before the teething period, a mere bath purifies the family persons of this Sootaka. If he dies after the tonsure ceremony has been completed the Sootak lasts for one night. For the one dying after the Yagya paneeta sanskar has been completed, the Sootak lasts for three nights. For a normal person dying after completing his Sanskar, the Sootak lasts for 10 nights. For daughters, the maximum duration of the Sootak is three days. Meaning that if some death has occurred in the married daughter's house, the affliction due to Sootak in her father's family lasts for only three days."

"During the Sootak period, formal worship of the deities is prohibited.

The king and the ascetic remain beyond the Sootak

affliction According to Manu, during a marriage ceremony should a death occur, the ceremony should take place, but the family members should not eat the food prepared before."

"O Garuda! I have formulated the system of Sampeedan[1] for each category, in accordance with the holy scriptures' injunctions. It is on the 12th day that the Sampeedan ceremony should be observed. The place where the deceased had died should be cleaned thoroughly and the area should be covered with the thin paste of the cow's dung. After ritually observing the Sampeedan the pinda thus created should be flown in the flowing water- river, canal or any water-course. Following this, the pious Brahmana should be given food and other things of use for a full month. One given Brahma should be appointed to receive the same."

"After this, on the 12the day the Dwadasha ceremony should be observed. The procedure is : on the 10th day the one who has conducted the last rites becomes pure; on the 11th he is accepted by his family or gotra people. On that day in Ekedasha they partake of food together to indicate the last rite performer's acceptance by his gotra. After the Sampeedan when the Dwadasha is observed, it signifies the last-rite's performer's final acceptance by the whole community, which confirms so by having food with him. On the eleventh day, 11 Brahmans should be fed on the choicest food, while on the 12th day, 12 Brahmans should be fed. Every day the family members should have their food only once in the day, that too after feeding the Brahmans.

"The bed of the deceased person or his other belongings should be given to only one Brahma on the 11th day. On the 13th day, 13 'padas' should be given to 13 Brahmans. Each pada should contain five things : an umbrella, a set of clothes, a pair of shoes, a kusha asava and a specified utensil filled with some sweet meat. This donation to 13 Brahmans ensures a smooth passage to the deceased person's subtle form till it reaches the Yama loka. All these things have their symbolical significance to this end. After Sampeedan and the Dwadasha, on every moonless day, till one year a Brahmana should he given (or fed) sweets, curds and fruits. This is called performing

---

1. In colloquid parlance it is also called 'Sapindee' which involves making the seven pindas (three generations from the father and three from the mother's side plus the deceased person) and mixing them together to form one Pinda.

51

the monthly Shraddha. In case, the additional month (Adhika-maas) falls in that year, the death anniversary should be observed only after 13 months. Thereafter, the Shraddha of the deceased should be observed on two days every year : on the person's actual death-day by the lunar calendar and on that particular tithi (the luner day) falling in the 'Pitnapaksha'! On the occasion of the Shraddha, the sandals (Khadaaoon of Vishnu, but symbolically two pieces of sandalwood) should be worshipped with the pollen of the plant basil. The Shraddha ceremony should be observed by the son or the descendants till someone in the family (Gotra) has performed the definitive shraddha in Gaya. Thereafter, there is no need to perform the Shraddha as the Gaya[1] Shraddha is supposed to ensure the deceased person's final release from the mortal bondage. In Gaya-Shraddha, the Pinda-Daan should be made while keeping a Shami leaf upon the head of a cow. This kind of Shraddha ensures the release of one's ancestor's soul from all mortal bondage."

"O Garuda! There is a garden near the Himalayas called the kalaap. It was the place the Pitra (manes) had recited a tale. According to which he who performs the Shraddha of his ancestors ensures not only salvation for their souls, but also for the final release of his own soul. This tale relates how Ishavaaku had performed the Shraddha of Manu. It says that those who respectfully give the donation of the pinda at Gaya have their progeny also following the righteous path. The performer of this Shraddha gets absolved of all their sins. The seven sons of Bhardwaaj who had even slain a cow were released from the affliction when their descendants performed the Gaya Shraddha for them. That is why I have narrated in detail this procedure and impressed upon you the importance of the Shraddha, particularly of the Gaya Shraddha. Now you may ask whatever you like for your enlightenment."

---

1. Gaya : A famous place in Bihar (now Jharkhand) which every Hindu must visit to ensure his ancestor's final release from the mortal bond.

12

The Realm of Yama

Garuda them asked Lord Narayan: "O Lord! Tell me in detail as to how big is the realm of Lord Yama and what sort of assemblies that take place in them and which kind of Dharma they support in their convention. Please also tell me as to which paths of faith should man follow to gain entry into those Dharma-Nagar assemblies?"

Lord Narain said: "A very good question you have asked and its answer ought to be revealed before all, including Narad and other sages. This Dharam Nagar is accessible to one after one's accumulating great minds. Located between the Yamapuri and the Rakshaspuri, the city of Yamaraj is very strongly built. No god or demon can break into it. It has been built this way: It is rectangular in shape, with 4000 kosa[1] long walls covering it from each of the four sides. Amidst the centre of it is located the Mandir of Chitragupta. The Mandir itself is 25 Yojan[2] with a 10 Yojan long iron boundary wall. Many flags flutter at its top. This Mandir resounds with beautiful music which enchants one and all. It contains many beautiful murals on its walls."

"Around the Mandir (temple) coo many sweet birds. The Gandharvas and Apsaras (divine dauseuses) keep on moving around it. Sitting in it, Chitragupta keeps the account of human beings' sanctioned age, and of their merits and demerits. It is he who decides as to which deed is meritorious and which is not. On the east of this temple is the building of deadly fevers. On the south is that of excruciating pains. On the west is that of the noose of Time and on the south is that of dyspepsia and other ailments. Due north is that of TB and jaundice. The Ishaan (north east) direction is that of headaches and Agni direction (south-east) that of syncope. So around this mandir in the basic form exists all righteous and non-righteous conducts of man and their consequences."

---

1. Nearly two miles by earthly unit of length.
2. Nearly eight miles by earthly unit of length.

About 20 yojan ahead of it is the temple (residence) of Yamaraj which is embedded with gems. This mansion shines like the sun and is spread to 200 yojan in area. It is 50 yojan high as well, supported by uncountable pillars. The resounding drums and bells keep reverberating in its surroundings. This unique mansion was wrought by Vishwakarma with his especial prowess."

"Inside this mansion exists a 100 yojan big divine assembly. It is nether very hot nor very cold, neither can enter it. Hunger or privation, with every kind of choicest food is always available. In it also exists a wish-fulfilling tree. This is, however, accessible to only those that are calm and truthful like the seasoned ascetics, the adept and those with long penance to their credit. It is in this divine mansion that the Lord Supreme sits on a 10 Yojan broad throne. All the high sages, adept, gods, and other divine personages ever remain in attendance here. All the great and illustrious kings and rulers like Muchikunda, Nimi, Ambreesha, Bhagirath, Sagar, Mandhata, Manu, Dilip, Prithir, Yayati, Nala, Shivi, Puru, Nahush, Pandu, Sahastra juma etc. - who proved their mettle in their jobs on the earth - remain here in attendance. They have all earned their right to grace this mansion.

This mansion or assembly house is such that those who enter it from the southern gate cannot see it. This citadel of Dharmaraj has four ways to enter it, though. The eastern gate is ever shadowed by the Parijaat tree and flanked by beautiful ponds, filled with nectar. This is the gate reserved for the entry of the gods, apsaras, huge snakes (like Shesha-naag), great adepts etc. Those who duly worship gods; the devotes of Lord Shiv, who donate water in the peak of summers and woods in the month of Magh (January); who help the poor and are truthful, who give pieces of land and the cows as alms; who listens to Puranas religiously and desist from committing unrighteous acts enter from this gate, without any difficulty. In fact, this is the gate reserved for truthful, honest and noble persons.

The second is the gate due north. It is always surrounded by many chariots, palanquins made of pure sandalwood. This is also a very conducive and pleasant way: sweetly shadowed and flanked by ponds filled with nectar.Those who welcome their guests with due respect; who read the Vedas, the devotes of goddess Durga and those that have much merit accumulated owing to their visiting all the holy teerthas and quitting also their mortal coils there only; the believers in the efficacies of the yoga discipline (the practitioners); those that honour Brahmans and remain faithful to their masters; those that make huge donations enter this city through this gate.

The third way to this city is through the way due west. That is also a well decorated and a shaded way, with the nectar ponds flanking it on both the sides. This way teems with the top elephants like the Indra's mount Eirawat and the top stallions like the Vclicheishrava. Those who have faith in the holy scriptures; who chant the Gayatri Mantra regularly; who are devotes of Lord Vishnu and are self-realised souls reach the Dharma (Yama) Raj's great mansion and the assembly through this gate only. Also those who are well learned, who don't incite or cause violence; who usurp nobody's share; who remain contented with their spouse; who are averse to worldly allurements, who feelingfully perform all the post-mortem duties toward their deceased ancestors: who duly discharge their familial duties and repay their dues and avoid the company of the wicked are also allowed access to the city through this west-gate. They reach the gate and imbibe nectar before proceeding to the Yama's Assembly.

When such noble beings reach the great Assembly, Yamaraj, adopting (Vishnu-like) his four-armed form, very lovingly welcomes them. After being welcomed these high souls are honoured by the Yama's hench persons. These beings are generally those that have realised the supreme being and eventually they have to merge themselves in Him only.

"As I have already told, those men with no faith and weak convictions go to hell. They are fools who even after getting this very rare human form fail to take advantage of it to improve their status in the divine realm. On the contrary, they further degrade themselves by getting drawn to worldly allurements. A man who follows the righteous and honest path not only improves his present life, but the status in the next, as well."

13

The Rebirth Procedure

Having learnt all details about the city of Yama or Yamapuri, Garuda again asked Lord Narayan: "Now Lord, Please tell me about those persons who dwell in the heavens. Having completed their term in heaven, are they again sent to the mortal world? Then, what families do they take birth in, what sort of thoughts do they have when they remain in their mother's womb before their next birth? Or, do they remain conscious?"

Lord Narayan said: "This question covers all aspects of this ocean of the soul's migration. I will explain it to you. After their term in heaven, they are again given a chance to improve their ultimate status. So they return to the earth. How they are conceived and what families they get in their next birth will now be narrated by me."

"Those with a positive credit to their ultimate account get birth in noble or good houses. They are conceived on the eighth day after the menses of their potential mother. The copulation on the eighth day ensures birth of sons. Thereafter the copulation on the even numbers of days results in the birth of a male child and on odd days, the daughters. According to the general tradition, the period when a women can conceive lasts for 16 days or nights. Copulation on the 14th day from the end of the menses goes to conceive a definitely religious and virtuous son. This kind of productive period is hardly available for any other species. The woman should have sweet edibles on the 5th day and refrain from eating bitter and astringent or spicy food. It is because the woman acts as a receptacle while the male seed as the germinating agency. On the given days the seed will have all nectarous qualities. It is only a good seed that results in the good crop. The male child conceived this way promises much righteous achievements in life. The son born this way will get the benefit of his Sanskars of the early life, as well which will goad him to do only auspicious deeds. In fact, one gate a good wife as a consequence of his previous life's noble deeds. Such a man always contemplates on the form of the Supreme Being."

Then, stressing on the right mix of the five elements that go in the making up of the embryos for such a person's conception, the Lord said: "O Lord of Birds! The elements of earth go to create in the human body the bone, skin, nerve, bristles and flesh and the saliva, urine, semen, tendons and blood are created by the water element. One feels hunger, thirst, lethargy, sleep and radiates with the glow of the visage by the element of fire. The element of air makes him capable of physical activities - like running, playing and jumping or skipping. The element of the sky creates in one's mind infatuation, suspicion, worry and the capacity to utter a word. Owing to the sanskaras inherited from the previous life, one gets one psyche, mind-set, the sense of ego or the general demeanour. In fact, all these four are collectively represented by the term called 'Autah-Karuna' or one's inner-self. The five sensory perception door are ear, skin, eye, nose and tongue which are called the 'gyanendriya'. The organs representing one's activity are speech, hands, arms, feet, the private organ. The Wind-god, directions, the Sun, the Prachitas, Indra, are supposed to be friendly deities to the Gyanendrias. The ten principal nerves called Irha, Pingala, Sushamna, Garndhari, Gajajihwa, Poorsa, Yashwasini, Alambusha and the tenth Shanphini control ten kinds of winds in the body, including Pran, Apan, Saman, Udaan, Vyaan, Naag, Koorma, Kripala, Devadutta and Dhananjaya. The wind Pran's realm is heart, Apan's anus, Saman's the stomach, Udan's the throat and Vyan in the rest of the body. The wind called Naag is released by a belch and the Koorma when one wakes up through the eyes - it is also called Urmeelan. The wind Krikala generates the hunger in the body. In yawning, is released the wind called Devadutt. The wind called Dhananjaya permeates the entire body, including the dead one. The food eaten in morsels nourishes the entire body in the following way. The wind Vyaan takes the essence of the eaten food to the nerves. These winds the entire ingested food this way into two broad sections - entering the anus region, these winds divide the undigested food into separate sections: the watery part and the solid undigested food. Thus, the body keeps on absorbing the ingested food by alternatingly keeping the fiery parts below and the watery part above. This way a heat wave is created which keeps on digesting the food and expelling the undigested food from the body through the anus and other extremities of the body. There are as many as twelve exit gates for body to expel unwanted material or 'Mala'. They are the ears, the eyes, the nose, the tongue, the teeth, the hand, the nails, the arms, the organ, the veins, the bristles and the skin. This way these watery, airy and fiery elements remain engaged in their work to keep the body healthy. O Lord of Birds! A human body has two forms: One practical (physical) and the other post-practical or the spiritual. The practical part has 350 millions bristles, 7 lakh hair and twenty nails. O Garuda! Normally a body has 32 teeth. A body is made up of 1000 Palas flesh (nearly 600 gm) and 100 Palas of blood. It has fat worth 10 Palas, 70 palas of skin, 12 Palas muscles and 3 palas Maharakta. The semen's total secretion could be 500 gms and corpuscles (red) about 250 gms. A body contains in all 360 distinct bones. It has a network of nerves, stretching to uncountable dimmesion. it contains 50 Palas bile and 25 Palas phlegm. There is no fixed quantity of the excreta and urine being created perpetually. This is the physical body.

Present in the spiritual or astral body of the humans are all the 14 Bhuvans (realm), mountains, islands oceans, the rivers and the plants in a symbolical form. It has 6 definite decision-circles. A human body contains every quality which is anywhere in the universe. All these facts are known to the self realised yogis or adepts. Now I describe to you its huge-sprawling-form."

"Below the feet is Tala, and that above them in Vitala. At the knee level lies 'Sutala' and at the joint of the organ is Sakthi-desh. At the base of Sakthi-tala is 'Talatala' and at the recess inside the organ is 'Rasatala' while at the waist level is 'Patala'. These are called the seven loka (realms) of the human body. The Bhooloka is at the navel, beyond it is Bhuvar loka. At the heart is Swarloka and at the throat is Maharloka. The Janaloka is at the mouth (inside), the Topoloka at the cranium and at the crown of the head is Satyaloka. There are 14 Bhuvans (levels). Around it are located seven mountain ranges. If the human body is likened to the earth, the Jambudweep is represented by the bones, the Shakadweep by the muscles, Kushadweep by the flesh and the Knoncha by the veins. The skin represents Shalmalidweep and the Gomeddweep; the nails and hair by Pushkardweep."

"Now I tell you about the oceans. The all pervading 'Virat Purush[1], has the oceans as his urine, the oceans of milk as his milk and of the muscles as ghee. The 'Rasa' is the ocean of relish and the curds as his blood. O Lord of the Birds! All sweet water reposes at his throat. The Sun is at his Naad-Chakra and the Moon at his Bidnu-Chakra[2]. Mars represents his eyes and Mercury his heart. Jupiter at his navel level and Venus at his seminary glands. Rahu is at his face level and Ketu at its external wind's level. This way, the whole of the human body is the tiny replica of the Virata Purush constituted this way. He who contemplates on his body as the representative of the 'Virat Purusha' symbolising the whole universe gets absolved from all the consequence of his sins."

Whereupon, Garuda asked : "Lord ! Tell me also about meditation in which without uttering any word a man is able to get above his physical consciousness."

The Lord said : "Manipooraka, Swadishthaan Anahat, Vishuddha, Mooladhar and Agya are the six Chakras. These Chakras has the following six forms.

1. The four petalled Mooladhar Chakra
2. The six petalled Swadhishthaan Chakra
3. The 10 petalled Manipooraka Chakra
4. The 12 petalled Anahat Chakra
5. The 16 petalled Vishudhha Chakra
6. The two petalled Agya Chakra

All these Charkras among them are believed to be the origin of 50 letters (of the Devanagani Sonipt). Beyond these is the 1000 petalled lotus chakra which is ever instinct with Lord Shiv and his Shakti. This Lotus is complete with an ethereal and unfading light."

"The scholars say that in one day and night one breathes for 21,600 times, with each breath chanting inaudibly the names of Ganesh (3000 times), of Hari (6000 times), of Hara (Shiv) (6000 times) and the remaining of Brahma, the Jivatma and one's Guru. This way one inaudibly chants the names of all the prominent gods."

Explaining the worship mode, the Lord said "First, a man should concentrate on his real faith - the ultimate objective in

---

1. Imagining the whole creation as his form.
2. The basic centre by the Yoga discipline's reckoning.

life. This should be followed by the chanting of the Gayatri Mantra as explained by one's Guru. Finally, he should concentrate upon all the Chakras mentally and try to awaken his hibernating basic power called the Kundalini lying dormant in three and a half folds and make an attempt to take it to the Brahmarandhra or the crown-point upon his head, because once the way is paved, his vital forces may exit through this passage to make the being attain the ultimate state - the place at Lord Vishnu's feet."

"In this entire meditative process, he must be guided by his guru. This way he may realise the ultimate power that his body is endowed with. Those ignorant who do not realise this body's basic strength and let it blossom fully, often fail to achieve their desired objectives. However, Garuda, the best way to ensure one's salvation is not these physical activities, but pure Bhakti - that is merging one's self with the Supreme Self.

14

The Ways to Salvation

Garuda said : "O Lord Narayana! You have now gracefully described how a being comes into the world. Please also tell me how anyone can attain Moksha (Salvation or the final releases), because this world is full of allurements which deviates one from reaching this aim. So O Eternal Lord! Please tell me as to how can one get this salvation?"

While elaborating on the fact that all beings come to the world at Lord Sadeshiv's inkling, the Lord said : "Now I tell you about the way that one can attain Moksha. First I tell you how a being graduates from the lower to the higher species."

"The lowliest birth is in the form of an inanimate object then ascent - tree - birds - animals - man in that order. Those humans who lead a righteous life get the divine specified in the next birth. The divinities is the final stage before a soul's salvation. There are in all four types of being : viviparous (Andaja); sprouting from beneath the ground (Udibhijja); sweat-born Swedaja) and egg-born (Andaja) A being repeatedly gets birth and death and only in their birth do some of them succeed to get the human form. And finally, it is a self-realised man who gets the final salvation after the soul's movement though most of the entire 84 lakh species. However, the human body has such a developed brain as could give the being or the soul the real knowledge of the existence. He who doesn't act righteously is in fact, a fool and a dunce who lets go his chance of improving his status in vain.

"Human effort is a great symptom of the brain's intelligence. Man must use this opportunity to earn more merit. But man shouldn't be infatuated towards his body which is fey. Instead he should try to contemplate on the Supreme Being through the medium of his Atma which is a rare source available to him. However, curiously enough, even a leper remains attached to his transient body. This way, most of the beings lose the rare opportunity given to them to improve one's general status at the overall count. Even though he sees the other fellow being committing the silly mistake, he learns nothing from them and keeps on repeating the same mistakes himself. He knows that this entire existence is so fickle as the bubble of water, but he still pays more attention to his physical fulfilment and not to his spiritual upliftment. Even the winds could be bound and the sky could be divided but it is impossible to rely upon the transient age. Time rules the roost here in his mortal world. No matter what one may plan, a single moment can upset one's entire planning. No mortal can escape the hands of time. This mortal world has a variety of potential griefs and he who gets above this physical world derives the real advantage of his human existence."

"The way a fish doesn't look at nail in the bait, but at the tempting food and thus gets at last hooked, the same way a man doesn't see the tortures awaiting him at Yamaraj's realm, but feels drawn towards the worldly delights."

"It is the bounded duty of all men to understand other faiths as well while sticking to his own in observing the Varhashram Viyavastha. It is my Maya which tests everyone's insight and those who see through it and doesn't deviate from their path eventually reach me. No matter what perances one accomplishes, but until one realises the basic objectives of human life, one cannot get over the sensual temptations. A real ascetic is who one doesn't as much care for his tendril locks or the deer skin but for this final realisation. No outward endeavors can take one to me. It is only the inner realisation that gives access to one to reach me O Garuda! He who is satiated by drinking nectar doesn't need any other diet. The same way, one who realises the secret of salvation and acts accordingly, doesn't need to worship ritually or live in the ordained conduct even." "Knowledge is believed to have two forms to enlighten oneself: One through the study of the books and holy scriptures and the other through acquired personal knowledge. But, the true knowledge is that which liberates. He who has this knowledge dawning on him doesn't fear death when he feels it approaching. In that situation, one should leave one's home and take bath in a holy teertha. Then wearing a deer skin, sit on a kusha-assana and start chanting the holy syllable of 'Aum or Onkar.' He must start feeling the communion with the Supreme Being by repeatedly calling: "I am him, I am him! He who sheds his mortal coil this way gets salvation and merges his soul with me."

Garuda asked again: "Which are those teerthas that one should go to when he senses his end approaching?" Lord

Narayana said: "The salvation bestowing teerthas are seven : Ayodhya, Mathura, Kashi, Gaya, Kaanchi, Avantika and Dwara Vati (Dwarika). Now I have told you all about the ways one may get salvation. What else do you want to know?" Garuda bowed repeatedly in reverence to the Lord and said: "Lord! Please also enlighten me on the ideal conduct that man should follow. What should he do to maintain a right conduct?" Lord Narayan said: "After getting knowledge from the Shruti (Vedas) and Smirit (personal experience), one should act truthfully, magnimaniously, with consideration for all, while following one's faith and doing the ritual worship as ordained by the scriptures. A Brahman should perform yagya and spread knowledge. A kshatriya should rule efficiently and ensure that no injustice is perpetrated during his rule. A Vaishya must honestly do his business without cheating anyone. The right conduct for a Shoodra is to serve the other three categories with full devotion."

"Secondly, each one of them must observe one's familial duties, satisfying one's all relations to the best of one's ability. Having done so, at about the time that one thinks that one has done so, one should leave the Grihastha Ashram and enter Vaanprastha Ashram in which he should get rid of worldly allurements and bonds totally to concentrate on one's spiritual upliftment. He must start living in the hermitages, taking advantages of the seers', knowledge and staying with them. He should fill his belly with whatever fruits etc. that he finds easily available. When he thinks that he has got over the worldly allurements, he must prepare to entire the fourth and final Ashrama called Sanyas, Ashrama. This is the stage when one sees the whole universe permeated with just one Existence. With the result, his relationship with every one-live or inanimate-becomes even. In this stage, he should not dwell even in the hermitages, but keep roaming about and relaxing during the nights beneath a tree. He must not save anything for the future and become indifferent to all the relations and identifications of the self. He must concentrate on the Realisation of the self." "This covers the various stages in general. However, amongst them the most difficult one is the Grihastha Ashrama. In this, he not only has to look after his worldly duties, but also to ensure that he doesn't neglect his truthfulness and piety."

"A Grihastha should take bath thrice in the day and each time it should be followed by Sandhya (The prayers at the truncation of the Day i.e. morning, evening and before the nightfall). For a Brahmachari, bath and worship once in a day is enough. In every worship, the following things or being should be given attention to: Brahmana, cow, the Kushasana, gold, ghee, the Sun, water and the ruler of the region. He must ensure that not only he, but all the members of the family, including the guests are well fed and well looked after. He must honestly earn his wherewithal."

"There are three ways that one could receive money: from the ancestral property, from some one, gifted out of love, the one received from the wife's side, from personal earnings, windfall, from the son and from the king. But for a Brahman there are only three avenues of getting money: from begging, from his knowledge or from donation. A Kshatriya (king) also gets it from three avenues: from the taxes; from the penalty (imposed upon other as the king) and the money won from the victory expeditions. The same way, a trader also has three sources; from agriculture, from business and from money as interest on investments. A king (Khatriya) could get help from them without any inhibition because this sort of counter financial service to the ruler carries no stigma."

"But every one should ensure that nobody is usurping anybody's share. One should live cleanly, taking bath every day and observing one's duty feelingfully and justly. From piety, point of view, however, there is much importance given to keeping vows. Particularly, keeping the fast on the Ekadashi day results in one's becoming the beloved of lord Vishnu. Moreover, he who desires the grace of Lakshmi must use 'Anwala' in clearing his body and taking bath every morning. When the time dawns for one's breaking fast, one should again take a bath and start his meal by taking sweet edibles. Then, he may have his salted cereal based food. Those items that have bitter, sour or pungent taste must be eaten in the end. The meal should always be washed down with milk."

"He who leads a life this way, doing all his jobs honestly and fulfilling all his duties honestly, eventually receives the highest state or Brahma pada when he quits his mortal coil."

15

The Diseases And Their Root Causes

Upon being asked by Garuda about certain diseases, Lord Narayan, said: "Now first listen from me about certain diseases as revealed by Dhanvantari. According to him, the 'Rakta-Pita' (mixture of bile with blood) is a very deadly disease, normally caused by consumption of very hot, spicy and bitter food. This mixture of bile with blood causes heaviness in the head. The patient doesn't like anything. It is accompanied by cought with wheezing sound in breathing. A foul smell keeps emerging from the mouth. It also causes a loss of vision and a man feels close to death. There is always a burning sensation in the mouth. Phlegm swells in he body. The patina feets as if needles are piercing his body all over the chest region. At this time the patient should have sweet things, like honey. In the chronic situation, the breathing trouble also starts with a shooting back-ache. An aggravated cought trouble leads to breathing problem as well. The wind travels in the reverse direction causing pain in the side of the heart. Heavy intake of food adds to the problem. Many times sleep gets disturbed. But when the patient is able to pass stool, he feels partially relieved. At times the patient feels like puking. Untreated, this problem even leads to the problem called hiccoughs, which is, according to Dhanvantari, also related to breathing. At times, eating something totally disagreeable to the body leads to this problem. The undesirable thing creates a sort of disturbance in the trapped wind, which leads to hiccoughs. This disturbed air can also cause faintness in one's cousciousness and spirit. Sometimes, it even leads to vomiting with a very loud noise. The patient himself feels as though there is some obstruction in his breathing."

"Thereafter, according to Dhanvantari, the Yakshma Roga (Tuberculosis) is a very deadly disease. This is also caused by very many reasons. But it is a highly enervating affliction. Previously, it used to afflict only the great kings. Hence, it is also called Raja-Roga (a royal disease). Generally, its reasons are four. First, the person's not caring about his diet and nourishment in the obsession of the work at hand. Irregular eating hours and not drinking fluids in adequate quantity is one of its major causes. The third reason is the body's losing its vitality due to some ulterior reason. Fourth is eating food without any distinctions. These four reasons agitate the bile which leads to weakness in the body and the Raja-Roga sets in. With the result the whole body acquires a palish look. Apart from the body ache, its other symptoms are seeing monkeys and snakes in the dreams and feeling very weak after copulation. Throat-ache, short of breath feeling, a pain that appears to break the body limbs etc. are its other symptoms. The patient blood becomes less owing to lack of its production in the body. This is a highly enervating disease.

The patient feels no appetite, with much burning sensation in the throat and palate. He or she may feel rather suffocated."

Sometimes excess discharge of the body-fluids leads to this problem. Excessive drinking of wine is also a cause for this Raja-Roga setting in in the body. Excessive strain on the body with over sweating of the glands is yet another cause of this trouble. The patient feels extreme dryness in the throat which even hampers one's breath."

"Normally, all these diseases afflict the body due to over agitation of the bile. Hence, a man should be regular about his eating habits."

"Sangrahani (dysentry) is also caused because of excessive depletion in the body fluids. This is also of four types. In the first case all the three basic humour of the body get disturbed. In the second case, one always feels thirty with a very unpleasant taste in the mouth. In the third case, one feels great burning sensation in the body, with ears resounding with a vibrating sound. Lethargy and languor make the patient lie listlessly. Curing the bowels is the best way to get cure from this trouble."

"This way, many serious diseases keep on afflicting the body and considerably reduce the person's sensory perceptions. Irregular food habits, excessive drinking of Varuni and other intoxicating fluids lead to many such diseases. One must shun such drinks and eat one's food at fixed hours to get relief from these ailments. While taking the treatment from the expert, the patient should also start doing certain specified yoga-asanas to keep the body fit."

Then dwelling on the treatment of the diseases, Dhanvantari, another incarnation of Lord Vishnu, said that to start treating any fever or disese, the patient should stop taking food. Instead, he or she should take only warm water, easily digestible fluids and stay in a less windy place. In case, the fever has been caused due to the foul wind, the patient should be administered the concoction (Karla) made of the mixture of the herb called 'Nagarmotha' and 'Giloy' (Both are very bitter herbs).

"If the fever is caused due to vitiating of the bile, a mixture of saunf (aniseed), motha and a fresh fruit should be administered. The Karha would help in the cure of this fever as well.

"Even the most severe fevers could be cured when giloy, Neem (leaves), Deodaru and Dhanyaka leaves are grounded with Triphala (Harar, Bahera, Anwala) and the paste is eastern mixed with honey. Eating Kateri, Nagarmotha, Gioloy, Pushkar, with Nagavalhi (serpentine creeper) Choorna (i.e. all of them reduced to a powered form) is a very effective dose to cure cough. This Choorna is better eaten with honey to give the best results." They dwelling upon the hair care, the Lord, quoting Dhanvantari again, said, "Even a bald person can get his hair back quickly if an ivory piece is reduced to powder form and this paste is applied on the pate mixed with little Anwala (myrobalan fruit). For general hair care adding the Gunja seeds' choorna, with the Bhringaraj juice and applying it regularly on the pate can ensure very soft and lush hair growth. Reduce to powder form the Bhringaraj seeds, a little of iron-dust, Triphala, Bijaura and Neela; mix the mixture with jaggery of even quantity and apply it on the head. This is a good dye to darken one's grey hair." "For ear care, take a little of anus urine, add a little of Saindhara salt (dark salt) and put a few drops in the ear at some fixed interval. This will not only keep the ears cleansed of the wax but shall also enhance one's hearing power. This is good for taking care of the oozing ear's problem."

"Add a bit of Shobharanjan leaves with even quantity of Madhu (honey) and apply it on your eyes to keen your eyes shining and trouble free." "Chewing the saffron seeds fortifies one's unstable or weak teeth. Eating the root of the Gunja creeper also strengthens one's teeth."

"A wound caused by any weapon is healed soon if the juice from the mango tree root is applied regularly on it."

Detailing further some tonics, the Lord said: "Remember that curds should not be consumed in cold and white season.

However, during Shishir, Hemant and rainy season they could be consumed. Taking a little of fresh butter, after meals, enhances glow on the face of the person. Take a little of Kushta powder and apply it with ghee and honey to get rid of the wrinkles on the face. Add a little honey wit pure sugar. Lick it and wash it down with unsweetened milk to strengthen your body. If one regularly applies Maloor-herb's juice, evenly mixed with water, on the hands, they become as strong as to stay unhurt even in a raging fire."

Giving a general advice, the Lord said: "These are some of the secrets that were revealed by Dhanvantri. One who follows the regimen suggested stays healthy for a long time."

16

Secrets of Pure Devotion

Them Garuda expressed his desire to learn the secrets of pure devotion to the Lord and the Lord obliged him the following way: "God deserves obeisance even though He may be called unborn, ummanifest and imperceivable. He who bows to God also becomes deserving to be reverened. He who chants 'Om Namo Navayamaya" and seeks refuge under Lord Vishnu has his welfare always assured. The turn 'Narayana' has infinitie capacity to incinerate one's sins. It is by constantly chanting this word that the high sages like Vyas and others have enhanced their discretionary wisdom. Those who sing together the prayers (kirtan) of the Lord become entitled for Moksha or salvation. Those that ever call: "O Achyta, O Anant, O Vasudena" and chant these names with great feeling never see the gate of the Yama's realm. The way the rising Sun destroy all darkness, the same way chanting the name of God destroys all sins. Even good deeds don't entitle one to reach this position, for they may take one to heaven, but only for a fixed period. Thereafter, they have to fall back into the ocean of births and death." Says Soota ji, "but those who chant the name of God with pure feeling keep on getting closer to the Ultimate abode of Lord Narayan. In Satyayuga concentrating one's mind above on God's form gets one a great reward, which one receives in Treta Yuga by worshipping God with all the parapherhelia. In Dwapar Yug Lord's ritual worship ensures great reward which one gets only by chanting Lord's name in Kaliyug. Lord is so great and kind that he who chants his name feelingfully gets entry to even his own realm." Continuing further, Soota ji enlightened the sages: "It is a universal fact that Lord Vishnu is the sole base of this entire universe. One gets no merit, no matter what holy teerthas one visits or accomplishes noble deeds, if one has no love for Lord Narayana. One salutation to Lord Narayan bestows merit equivalent to one's performing 60,000 Yagyas and visiting 7000 teerthas. No matter wilingly, or unwillingly, consciously or unconsciously, if one chants God's name one gets all that one desires. In fact, the ultimate

69

essence of every faith is concentrating on God's name. The utterance of His name makes available the rarest reward, should one desire. That time is wasted in which one doesn't think of God. He who has the image of Lord Narayan firmly imprinted in his heart can achieve even the impossible."

Saying further, Soota ji said: "One gets salvation if one could have the same intensity of devotion for God as a sensual person has for various sensual delights, one's salvation becomes a certainty. Like gold gets purged of all its impurity when passed through fire, the same way a man is cleansed of all his sins when he chants the name of Lord Vishnu. A regular worship of Lord Vishnu takes the devotes to the status of even Indra."

Alluding to Lord Vishnu's instruction to Garuda, Soota ji said: "He who, despite being a family man, keeps his mind concentrated on Lord Vishnu, stays away from the illusion of the worldly legerdemain thrown upon the creation by the Divine powers. He continues to be full of the milk of human kindness and considerate to the entire creation. This way, he stays clean. Those that have their mind concentrating on Lord Vishnu's form don't go to hell. Those who surrender themselves unto the supreme being get salvation."

Then dwelling upon the ordained duty of the king, the Lord says: "A king is the patron of his people. He protects them the same way as parents protect their children. Remember that if one follows one's religious faith with a total faith he gets protected only by that faith. For it prevents the person froms treading the unrighteous path. And there is no condition as to who should he the Lord's devotee. One could be of lowly caste, even a pariah, but if he devotedly worships Lord Vishnu one stays clear of all the profanities and becomes the Lord's dear. He whose hands don't devotes themselves in the Lord's worship, whose feet don't visit the Teerthas dedicated to Lord Vishnu, never face any defect in life. Even the insects and lowly beings get higher status in life if they could get the God's grace. It is the ultimate objective of any live being to draw the attention of Lord Vishnu. He who manages to do so gets the highest status when he quits his mortal coil."

Soota ji said: "It is really amazing that despite having the cool shade of Lord's worship available, men still burn himself in the scorching fire of the world and suffer hells and the allied tortures."

Concluding his narration, Soota ji said: "O sages! Now I

70

have disclosed before you the Bhakti of Narayan and all the attended benefits: Now, how Narayan ensures his devotee's welfare is explained through the narration of an episode. It had been described by Lord shiv While his hymning Lord Narsimha."

"Once Lord Shankar was told by his one 'Gana' (hench person) that: "Lord By your grace we can devour any god, demon or man. Hearing this, Lord Shanker advised him to perish such a wicked thought. Protect all the beings for that is what you are here for."

"However, those hench persons refused to abide by their Lord's advice and they started to recklessly devour the creation. When the chaos created by Lord Shiv's hench persons became uncontrollable, Lord Shiv himself invoked Lord Vishnu's Narsimha form in the following way. O Lord! You have no beginning or end. You are the origin of the entire creation. You have a tongue that flashes like lightning. Your jaws are all-devouring and your powerful neck is covered by a garland full of the precious gems. You have a dazzling crown reposing upon your head. A lovely gold cummerbund is tied round your waist. You have a dazzling dark complexion. A pair of bejeweled anklets are gracefully placed around your feet. Your whole body is full of the round-bristles that look comely like innumerous whirlpools. Covering your large bosom, a beautiful garland. Please come to put this chaos in order."

When Lord Shiv feeling fully invoked lord Narsimha, the Ultimate Lord in the Man-lion form put in an appearance before Lord Shiv. Bowing before him, Lord Shiv again hymned his praise and called him the Lord with deadly nails who tore apart the ferocious demon Lord Hiranyakashyapa; the master of the universe and capable of subduing even Lord Yama. Alight with the glow of the thousand moons and repository of all divine wealth like Kubera, You, Lord, have been hymned by every Brahma, the creator, in every age. You are the sole Lord that can ensure total salvation to your devotees."

Then Lord Shiv said: "O Great Lord! The terrible hench persons that I created to slay the demon Andhaka are recklessly devouring the entire creation. Since I have created them, I am not entitled to cause their extinction. Since I am unable to destroy then, I request you to end their existence."

When this way Lord Shiv repeatedly requested Lord Narsimha, the latter extended his deadly tongue and destroyed all the vile henchpersons of Lord Shiv by the blow of the

71

fraction of his tongue's tip. This way, redeeming the earth, Lord Narsimha disappeared."

Said Soota ji "Whosoever reads this Narsimha strotra gets redemption from this cycle of births and deaths, with all his ambitions realised. Whosoever concentrates on Lord Nrishimha's red-lotus-like-brilliant eyes has all his sins duly atoned for and he gains the best status in the Vaikuntha lok." After this, Soota ji referred about the Acchuta Strotra, but preceding it with the narration of an anecdote. He said he learnt it from Narad himself."

Once Narad ji asked Brahma: "Please tell me about Acchuta Strotra so that ritually saying it I can propitiate Lord Vishnu. Also guide me in saying it correctly.

"Brahma ji said: "This Strotra forms the basis of Lord Vishnu's worship. Chanting it the man has his nook in the Lord Realm irretrievably reserved. This is like this: (A man should say)

- I bow to Lord Vasudeva!
- I bow to the Lord Capable of destroying all my sins!
- I bow to the Lord's Boar form!
- I bow to the Lord Govinda (master of Skies)!
- Lord! Your are omniscient and bestower of the eternal knowledge. I bow to You!
- Your the Supreme Indivisible Entity. I stand bowed in your service!
- You are the Creator, Sustainer and Destroyer of this entire creation. O Master of Universe, accept my Salutations!
- You are the creation's Manifest form. My salutations!
- O Destroyer of the Demon Madhu! My salutations!
- O The One having Garuda imprinted on his Flag; O Lotus-eyed!
- A Krishna you destroyed the demon called Kaliyanemi
- O son of Devaki and Espouse of Lakshmi! I bow to you, the scion of the Vishnu family (or Krishna)!
- O Beloved of the cow boys of the village Gokula, I salute in your Honour!
- O the Lifter of the Mount Goverdhan and who made the cows thrive with strength and vitality, I bow to you!
- O The Reality Manifest in the entire world, the Bestower of al that is noble and useful! I bow to you!
- You are Madhava, the Authority on the Vedas, the Omnipotent Lord of Lakshmi, I bow to you!

72

- You are the truth. The good, The Bliss - the sole repository of all knowledge! Victory to Thee, Victory to Thee, Victory to thee!
- O Unmanifest But all pervading Existence, my salutations to you!
- You are the Guru that dispels all ignorance and the fount of all the Holy Mantras! I bow to you!
- You are Time and Space! I bow to you!
- You are the Righteous flow of Time, my salutations to you!
- You are at once beyond of and instinct with all Maya, my salutations to you!
- You are the Deity wielding the conch shell, the Discus, the Mace, I bow to you!
- You, the Guardian of all Directions, I bow to you.
- You are also the Master of the devious; You are the wind and the Moon, My salutations to you.
- You are the twelve Adityas, both Ashwanikumaras and the Marudganas and Vasus - revealing yourself in myriad form, I bow to you!
- You are the (master of all) the giants, Naags, Gandharvas, Apsaras, the manes and the adepts, I bow to you!
- Nothing save you, Lord, exists in the whole creation, I salute you!
- You as the master of all the emotions of the heart that issue from the mind, prudence and egoistic identity! I salute you.
- You are the Yagya, the Om-kaar; the oblations and the offerings! I bow to you!
- O lord Supreme! You are the altar, the initiation and the holy fire! I convey my deep reverence to you!
- Lord ! You are the upsivinging holy smoke and the gratulatory songs! you are Man Par Excellence, all the Directions including the skies above and the land below, the constellations, the stars and the plants - you are Everything! I bow to you!

(He who chants this Strotra gets reduced from all the sins and learns about the true nature of Supreme Being who is perceptible, not even by infinite births in the various species. He who is said to be Imperceptible by senses and the Unknowable!)

"He is the pristine form of Brahma - the Being Primal and

Supreme! The All Pervading, beyond the Beginning or the end. Eleternal and Manifest, as well as Unmanifest, both. He alone is Omniscient, Fearless, Transcendental and bliss!

"I seek your pardon for all my lapses and do all my works deeming them as yours! I have my unwavering devotion to your feet! Day in and day out I worship you alone. I have no greater faith in any other belief - than your lotus-like feet because I believe this is the sole medium to ensure my salvation. You are the solitary bestower of all the fruits to my endeavours and their final success!"

This way, Soota ji said, saying this Grand Strotra Creator, the Brahma establishes the supremacy of Lord Vishnu. Worship him, the bestower of all the desired objectives. One should chant this Strotra early in the morning to have one's desire fulfilled and his place in the Vaikuntha assured.

17

An Interlude[1] :

The Allied Details and Stories

In this part we intend to give all the ancient information and details about leading life as was prevalent when this Purana was compiled.

Some Vastu-Details : (House Building Details)

First of all, the foundation stone laying ceremony should be observed. The thirty-two gods (deties) who should be observed on this day are : Ishana, Parjanya, Jayanta, Indra, Surya, Bhrigu, Aksha, Vayu, Pusha, Vithala, Grahanakshtras, Yama, Gandharva, the King of the region, the deer, the manes, the saltines, pushpadanta, Ganesh (the first to be worshipped), Asura, Shesha, Roga (the diseases' head) Soma, Aditi and Diti; the Goddess, the family deity, the Manudganas. Inside the premises of the house, one worships the four Gods called Apaha, Sanitra, Jaya and Rudra.

A temple should always be built in front of the house. Gates and doors and the places for performing the sacrifice should be due east. The north should be reserved for a store house. A pond should be towards the east and the guest house toward the south. In order to find whether that house will prove lucky or not, multiply the length and the breath of the area of the plot and divide it by eight. If the remainder is an odd number (till 8) the house will be lucky. In the case it is even, the area will prove unlucky. If even, some area should either be extended or subtracted from the plot.

Temple Building : A temple should have one, three or five spires. There are five types of temples; Vairaja, Pushpaka, Kailasa, Malaka and Tripishtapa which are respectively square, rectangular, circular, oval and octagonal in shape. There could

---

1. Only those detils that are not repeated in the other Puranas hve been called fcr this chapter in the form of a brief summary.

be a variation, but within these five basic shapes.

Near the temple should be a 'Ranga-Shala' (a stage) where plays could be enacted on the holy occasions. The temples must always be surrounded with flowers and fruit bearing plants and creepers. There must also be a water-course or a well to ensure uninterrupted supply of water.

The Duties in each Varna (caste or category)

(i)   Brahmana : perform sacrifices, donate alms, study and teach the holy Vedas (or other knowledge)

(ii)   Kshatriya : Protection of his people, donate alms and study martial arts apart from the other basic knowledge.

(iii)   Vaishya : Ensuring supplies and running business, donating alms and studying the practical knowledge; doing farming.

(iv)   Shoodra: Serving all, earning living by their physical skill - as artisans and helping in manual work at the fields, producing cereals etc.

All should live a life in four parts : in Brahmacharya for the first twenty-five years; in the Grihasthi (family) for the next twenty-five years; in Vanaprastha stage for the next twenty-five years and in Sanyas (as hermits) for the next twenty-five years. This way, the human life span is believed to be of 100 years.

All must get up at the stroke of dawn. After thinking of Vishnu, they must observe their self-cleansing rituals, including a bath. Bath has four varieties; Brahma-chanting the mantras and sprinkling water on oneself; 'agneya' - to rub one's body with ashes; 'vayavya' to rub one's body with cowding; 'varuna' - having a vigorous water bath; 'Yougika' - having bath for each limb of the body and 'Divya'- to have sun bath.

Teeth should always be brushed while facing the east.

All must donate alms or 'Daan-dena'. This is also of four kinds: Nitya, Nainilheka, Kamya and Vimala. Nitya is donating alms to Brahmans, without expecting anything in return. Nainilhika is the donation made with some specific objective, particularly for safeguarding oneself from various ill-omens or troubles. Kamya daan is made for having some desire related to progeny fulfillment. Vimala 'daan' is made for simply pleasing the Almighty.

He who gives sweets, cereals, cattle and lands to Brahmans earns great chances for attaining salvation. A sinner who restrains others from donating alms is born as a bird in his next life.

Prayaschita (repentance) means atoning for one's sins. The worst sin is killing a Brahmana. Staying in exile for twelve years, even immolating oneself or commiting suicide are some of the punishments that one should award to oneself in the 'Prayachita'. However, if one fasts for three days and nights and bathes regularly at the holy Sangam at Prayag, one may be reduced from this deadliest sin's consequences.

A person who dies at the holy teertha has automatically had his sins atoned for.

Physiogrnomical observations

Anyone having soft feet which don't sweat will become a king. A kingly person should have round thighs, with much little bristles on the body. Each pore of his body will have only one hair.

A poor person is he who has rough nails and hard feet. He will be flat footed. Each pore of his body will have one than one hair or bristle. A scholar should have two bristles emerging from his every pore on the body.

A person with three lines on the forehead may live for 60 years, with two 40 and with one, 20 years. But if there are three lines right across one's forehead, the person will live for 100 years.

A woman with a round face brings prosperity to the house that she goes to after marriage. But a woman with round eyes may become a widow. If there are many lines on her palms, it means that she will suffer from poverty. A chakra-sign on a woman's part foretells her either producing or marrying a king. She with shining teeth will never suffer want of food and she with soft skin and delicate lips will get a cosy bed to sleep on.

A man with a long nose has a fortunate existence. A person with a bent nose is evil and if it tilts towards the right, he will be a thief as well. One who speaks with a nasal tone lives long. Sinners generally have cat-like eyes. A man with symmetric eyebrows is a fortunate person. Also unfortunate is the man who cries without visible tears. If the life line on a woman's hand is thick, she will produce many sons. However, if the line is thin, she will have more daughters. Those with a long and unbroken life-line (the line almost encircling the thumb) indicates a long life.

In ancient India, foretelling one's fortune by looking at one's physique is called physiognomy.

The story of the Jewels origin

There was a demon called Balasura. With his observing difficult penance, he became invincible. He also defeated the Gods. In order to get back their lost capital, the gods arranged a yagya. Then, under the guise of a priest, they went to the Asura and demanded his body for the, oblation. Generous as he was, he decided to accede to the feigned priest's, request.

They took his body into an aerial vehicles (Vimana) which travelled as fast as to make the body fall off. As it hit the ground, it disintegrated into many parts. These tiny part, owing to that demon's commitment to the gods, became the jewels wherever they fell.

The Prominent jewels are: Vaja (diamond or Heeraka) Mukta (pearl), Mani (ruby), Marakata (emerald), Pushparaga (Topaz); Indraneela (blue sapphire or Neelam): Sphatika (crystal or moon-stone), Praval (coral or Moonga). A hexagonal diamond brings great good fortune to the wearer. Pearls can be obtained from eight sources including the elephant's head, clouds, boars, conch-shell, fishes, oysters and bamboos. However, oysters are the most common source. If a pearl needs to be polished, the Purana suggests a typical method. It says: "Put it inside the stomach of a pearl. Cover the fish with clay and roast it. The pearl should be taken out, to be washed with milk, wine and water in that very order. The pearl will become bright and shinning. In order to test whether the pearl is genuine or not, keep it sunken in saline water for a night. Then dry it. If its color doesn't fade, it is a genuine pearl."

Telling about the origin of the Vaidurya Mani (beryl or the Cats' eye) the Purana says that Balasura had roared before he died. His powerful roar had fragmented a part of the hill called Vidura. The pieces of it are known as Vaiduryamani. The Purana also claims that Ruby- the gem had originated from Balasuras's blood, the Emerald from his bile, the Sapphire from his eyes and the Topaz from his skin. This way, most of the gems had originated from the parts of that demon's body-limbs and fluids.

The Teerthas and the Story About the Hallowed Teertha Gaya

Teertha literally means any place located on the banks of the holy rivers. That is why Haridwar, Prayag and Gangasagar are very holy teerthas. Varanasi and Mathura are eternal abodes of Lord Vishnu and Lord Shiv. They become more sacrosanct because of their association of the two Super Gods.

Other famous teerthas are Prabhasa (west coast), Divarika, Saraswati (on the bank of this extinct river) and Kedara - the place on the Himalayas, the beloved spot of Lord Shiv. The teertha Badrinath is also very hallowed, due to its association of the twin seers: Nara and Narayan - the incarnations of Lord Vishnu, Gaya - a place now in Jharkhand - is a specially sacred teertha, particularly for the final oblations made by the descendants of the dead. How it acquired so much importance in the post-mortem ritual ceremonies is revealed through a story given below.

Aeons ago, there used to be a demon named Gayasura. He performed such difficult penances that even the gods felt panicky, the might in aspiring to usurp the divine throne. They so sought Vishnu's counsel to subdue this Gayasura. Vishnu advised them patience and promised to do something about it.

Once Gayasura had gone to collect some lotus flowers for his prayers. His exertions made him feel very tired. So he fell asleep. Seizing his opportunity, Vishnu came and killed him with his mace. This happened in the land known as Kikata. Where Gayasura's body fell on this region came to be known as Gaya. Since Vishnu himself had killed the demon it became a special seared place for performing the Shraddha of the departed beings.

Four methods are specially earmarked for the salvation of human beings. The first is the knowledge of the Supreme Being or the Brahma, the second a Shraddha ceremony at Gaya, the third is death in a cowshed and the fourth is dwelling on the plains of Kurukshetra.

Highlighting the importance of the Shraddha ceremony performed at Gaya, there is an interesting story which is given below.

There was a merchant named Vishala. The merchant had gone to Gaya and had performed a ceremony for his late ancestors. In the next life, the merchant was born a prince and got the same name. One day, Vishala saw a white being, a red being and a black being in the sky.

Curious, he asked them who they were. The white being said: "I am your father. Because you performed a ceremony for me in Gaya, I now dwell in heaven. The red being is my father, that is your grandfather. He had commited a sin of

79

killing a Brahmana. But, because of the ceremony you performed at Gaya for us, he too now lives in heaven. The black being is my grandfather and your great grandfather. He had committed the sin of killing a sage. But thanks to the ceremony you performed in Gaya, he too lives in heaven now." Indeed, the ceremony performed at Gaya absolves the whole lineage of its misdeeds.

Marriages and Cross - Breeds

The bride and the groom should not have any blood ties with each other, upto the ninth (some versions of this Purana say seventh) generation on the father's side, and upto the seventh (some versions of this Purana claim upto third) generation on the mother's side. Brahmans, Kshatriyas and Vaishyas should have no matrimonial alliance with the Shoodras. However, a Brahmana groom can marry a bride from the Kshatriya and Vaishya categories, apart from his own. A Kshatriya groom is allowed to marry a Kshatriya or a Vaishya bride. A Vaishya groom should only marry a Vaishya bride and a Shoodra groom should only marry a Shoodra bride. In certain condition, however, Pratiloma (from lower to the higher category) is permitted. Anrioma marriage is not prohibited in general.

There are many types of marriage. Their details are as follows:

1. **Brahma Marriage :** The groom is invited and is given a bejewelled bride.
2. **Daiva Marriage :** When a daughter is given to the Priest of a yagya as a gift.
3. **Arya Marriage :** In this, two cows are accepted from the groom as bride-price and the bride is then handed over together with these cows.
4. **Prajapatya Marriage :** In such a marriage, a bride is handed over to a groom with the words: "Together the two of you should perform your religious duty or Dharma."
5. **Asura Marriage :** This marriage is held when the bride's price has been duly paid.
6. **Gandharva Marriage :** When the bride and the groom fall in love with each other and get married, this marriage is consummated. It has no conditions attachments.
7. **Rakshasa Marriage** The bride is kidnapped by the

groom and married. But, she must be willing for such a union.

8. **Paishachik Marriage:** The bride is forcibly abducted and married, even though she may be totally unwilling for this union.

Among these, the first four categories of the marriages are recommended for the Brahmans, the next two for the Kshatriyas, apart from the first two, the Asura marriage for the Vaishyas and the last one only for the Shoodras.

However, despite injunctions to the contrary, Brahmana grooms have got married to Kshatriyas, Vaishyas and Shoodra women. This has led to birth of cross-breeds. The son of a Brahmana father and a Kshatriya mother is called "Murddhabhi shikta"; the son of a Brahmana father and a Vaishya mother an "Ambashtha, the son of a Brahmana father and a Shoodra mother a "Nishada", the son of a Kshatriya father and a Vaishya mother is called "Mahishya", the son of a Kshatriya father and a Shoodra mother an "Ugra", The son of a Vaishya father and a Shoodra mother is known as "Karana".

The offspring of a Brahmana mother is called 'Suta' if the father is a Kshatriya. 'Vaidiha' if the father is a Vaishya, and 'Chandala' if the father is a shoodra. The offspring of a Kshatriya mother is called 'Magadha' If the father is a Vaishya and 'Kshatta', if the father is a shoodra the progeny from a Shoodra father and Vaishiya mother is called 'Ayogava'.

The term for cross-breeds in Sanskrit is 'Varna-Sankar.'

The sequence of Rebirth for the sinners

After having paid for some of his (or her) sins in the hell (Naraka), the sinner has to be born again in this mortal world. The killer of a Brahmana is first born as a dog, then progressively as a camel, a donkey, a frog and an owl. The stealer of gold is reborn as a worm or an insect. A person who steals food starves in his next life. A liar becomes dumb in his next life. A stealer of oil is born a as cockroch and a stealer of green vegetables as a peacock. A stealer of fruits is born as a monkey; a stealer of animals as a goat, a stealer of milk as a crow; a stealer of fragrant substance as a mole, a stealer of food grains as a rat; a stealer of animals as a goat, a stealer of milk as a cow; a stealer of meat as a vulture and the stealer o clothes gets only torn clothes to wear in his next life. This way, each receives the next birth in accordance with his deeds or misdeeds performed in the previous life.

The Regimen for Vratas:

These Vratas (the fasts) are observed partly as atonement for the evil deeds and partly for getting more religious merit accrued to one's credit. The Vratas for each tithi (lunar dates) are given below.

1. Pratipada (1st lunar day): A fast observed and the God of life is propitiated for wealth.

2. Dwiteeya (2nd lunar day) : A fast is observed and Yama, Lakshmi and Vishnu are propitiated.

3. Triteeya (3rd lunar day) : Fast is observed to propitiate Lord Shiv and Parvati.

4. Chaturthi (4th lunar day): Fast is observed to propitiate the Lord of Obstructions, Ganesh.

5. Panchami (5th lunar day): Fast is observed to propitiate Lord Vishnu.

6. Shashthee (6th lunar day): Fast is observed to propitiate Lord Kartikya.

7. Saptami (7th lunar day) : Fast is observed to propitiate Lord Sun.

8. Ashthami (8th lunar day): Fast is observed to propitiate Goddess Durga.

9. Navami (9th lunar day): Fast is observed to propitiate the Undecayable Lord Vishnu.

10. Dashmi (10th lunar day): Fast is observed to propitiate Lord Moon and Yamaraja.

11. Ekadashi (11th lunar day): Fast is observed to propitiate Lord Vishnu and the high sages. On this day eating rice is particularly prohibited.

12. Dwadashi (12th lunar day): Fast is observed to propitiate Vishnu and the Moon.

13. Triyodashi (13th lunar day): Fast is observed to propitiate the God of love Anang or Kamadeva.

14 Chaturdashi (14th lunar day): Fast is observed to propitiate Lord Shiv.

15. Poornima (Or Amavasya): Fast is observed to propitiate both the Sun and the Moon Gods.

Apart from these, on weekdays the worship table and the fast regimen is given below:

Sunday - Sun; Monday, Moon or Lord Shiv; Tuesday - Kartikeya and Lord Hanuman; Wednesday - Vishnu and Ganesh; Thursday - Ganesh and Jupiter (Brihaspati), Venus - lord Shiv and the Sage Bhrigu; Saturday - Saturn and the Lord Hanuman.

Besides, there maybe days warranting special worship of the particular God - like during Navaratra - Goddess Durga; Janmashthami - Lord Krishna (Vishnu); Ram Navami - Lord Ram (Vishnu); Shivratri- Lord shiv; Ananta Chaturdashi - Lord Shesha Naag. etc. This way, apart from the general worship, there are particular days for various deities worship. The consequences of not doing so has already been explained in the preceding chapters.

There is, however, a special Vrata period called Bishmapanchaka. This was the day in the month of Kartika when the Grandsire of Mahabharat fame, Bheeshma fell in that great war. The grateful Hindus faith observes the five days in sympathy for him. It starts on the bright lunar day, on Ekadashi Tithi and continues upto Poornima. During this period, first the ancestors - starting from Bhishma are worshipped, then Vishnu's image is bathed in Ganga Jal and is duly worshipped. The first day, the offerings are made of flowers which are placed on the image's (or icon's) feet. The second day on the thighs; the third day on the navel; the fourth day on the shoulders and the fifth and final day on the head. It is a symbolic gesture; praying for Bhishma's redemption from pain in the given part of the body on the particular day.

Throughout these five days, the devotee has to sleep on the floor, eating only Panchagavya (the five products yielded by a cow).

Medical Treatment: Dhanvantari, the fount of all the Ayurvedic knowledge and believed to be the incarnation of Lord Vishnu who appeared after the ocean churning with the pitcher of nectar on his hands, has also made enough contribution to this Purana. Some of the details about the various diseases have been given in the previous chapters. Here, we shall deal with only the method of medical treatment.

There are five steps to any medical treatment. The first is Nidaan (or diagnosis). On the basis of Unmanifest symptons, this spills over into 'Purva roopa', that is, when the first symptoms start appearing. Next is roopa when the symptoms are fully manifest. The fourth stage is called 'Upashaya'. This involves the treatment of the disease through medicine, diet and other regimens. The final stage is called 'Samprapti' which means recovery of the normal health.

The recommended herbs and creepers, roots and bulbs for making medicines to treat a variety of diseases (some of them

83

have already been hinted) are: Priyangi (black mustard seeds), Godhuma (Wheat), Pippali (pepper plant) Madhu (honey), Bilva (wood-apple), Eranda (Castor) Sarshapa (mustard Yellow), Padma Patra (lotus leaves); Kaksharah (a lentil also called Khesari), Palanka (Spinach), Dadima (Pomegranate), Kesar (saffron); Matulunga (a very sour variety of bitter lemon), Anwala (myrobalan fruit or leaves); Panasa (jack-fruit), Khajura (dates), Adraka (ginger), Heenga (asafoetida), Saindhara Namak (rock-salt); Ghrita (ghee or clarifed butter), til (sesame seeds), Ikshu (Ganna or sugarane), Triphala (a mixture of Harash Baaheda, Anwala), Takra (clarified whey), Yashthimadhu (licorice), Ashwagandha the physalis flexuose plant), neela (indigo), Yavakshara (nitrate of potash), Shankara (sugar), Haridra (turmeric); Lashuna (garlic), Musta (fenugreek), Shririsha (minosa), Ila (cardamom), Chandana (sandalwood), Deodaru (pine tree products), Hastidanta (ivory), Laksha (lac), Palash (the tree butea fondosa), Tambula (betel leaf), Lavana (salt) , Jambu (Jamun) and the herb called Punarnava. Punarnava is a very potent herb, capable of reviving life or overhauling the entire body with a fresh vitality. It is said that under the Pushya Nakshatra (the 8th lunar asterism), this herb should be crushed and its juice to be drunk with water. This esures not only the snakes and other poisonous insects, having no effect on the body, but it almost reviews the body for the next year.

Treatment for the weak Horses and Elephants

A short-eared horse lives long. If Mustard, Ghee, sesame, asafoetida and a piece of wood are tied in a small piece of cloth around the horse's neck, its general welfare is assured. Castor-oil, turmeric, garlic, and rock salt-meshed and mixed together into a paste make a very effective remedy for the wounds on a horse's body. Whatever medicines are used for a horse's treatment can also be used to treat an elephant, but the quantity should be quadrupled. In case an elephant falls sick, apart from the medical treatment, Brahmans should also be fed and jewels donated along with the cows to ensure their quick recovery. Tieing a garland around an elephant's tusk and throwing mustard seeds charged with the mantra also help in their quick recovery.

Yoga and the True Knowledge

The union of the Atman (soul) with the ultimate soul

(Parmatma) is called Yoga. All sages ultimate aim is to achieve this union, which dawns upon one, the Ultimate or True knowledge. But before this union can be achieved, the intelligence, the mind and the senses have to be controlled and concentrated on meditating on 'Brahman' (the Supreme Being). There are six techniques of Yoga. These are known as : Pratyahara, Japa, Pratyahara, Dhyana, Dharana and Samadhi. Pranayam means breath control; Japa means chanting the holy Mantra; Pratyahara means control over one's senses; Dhyana means meditation on the chosen subject, Dharan means continuous and focussed Dhyana and Samadhi means getting into the trance while thinking on the chosen subject. Samadhi occurs which the object of meditation is seen everywhere. It is the stage when the union of the Atman and Parmatman is finally achieved. This coalescence issues forth the true or ultimate knowledge. One feels as though one has woken up from a deep slumber. One realises that Atman has nothing to do with grief or gratification, weal or woe in a worldly life. Once the smoke of illusion is cleared, the glow of the hidden Self in self blazes forth in the full glory.

The Vrishotsarga Tale

An referred to in the 10th chapter, much significance is attached by this Purana for donating a healthy and blemishless hull on the 11th day or the Ekedasha day. Once there ruled a king named Viravahana in the city called Viradha. One day the great Sage Vashishtha came to visit him. Having duly welcomed him, the king asked: "Tell me, great sage how can our avoid going to Yama's realm and escape suffering tortures there?"

Vashishtha said : "The learned have described that by donating a bull, one can escape the visit to Yama's realm. You must follow the example of Raja Dharmavatsa."

"Who was Raja Dharmavasta?" the king asked and the sage recited the following story.

Dharmavatsa was a Brahmana living in a city called Vidiha. Once he went to a hill to fetch some sacrificial grass. While he was still searching for it, four handsome men came and grabbed the Brahmana. They rose high up into the sky and began to carry him far away. Soon they arrived at a city with many gates and palaces.

The Brahmana was confused as to where and why he had been kidnapped. Or whether it was just an illusion. By then, he had been placed before a golden throne with a king seated on it. Seeing Dharmavastu, the king started to worship him with a variety of offerings.

"Today, I am really blessed, said the king. I have now seen you, a great soul." Then he ordered his men to take him back. Dharmavastu was bewildered "Wait a bit, I say", he interrupted. "Will you please explain as to why have I been kidnapped and why I am being sent back. What is the purpose behind these mysterious happenings.

"I love to set my eyes on those that deserve to be worshipped. You are a very righteous fellow, one who worships Lord Vishnu. Please pardon my impertinence. Why did I do so is what my minister will tell you." His minister was Vipashchit. He told Dharmavastu the following story.

In an earlier life, the king had been a king, living in the city of Viradha. His name was Vishambhara and he was a Vaishya. H was a very pious and god-fearing man. He had a beautiful and an equally pious wife. Although he was a very honest and righteous person, he was still attached to material possessions. In order to get rid of these infatuations, he decided to visit all the holy teerthas and acquire a divine vision. In one of the teerthas, he happened to meet sage Lomash. Learning about the purpose of the Vaishya's pilgrimage, the sage said : "Once Narad had also developed this kind of infatuation. No matter what he did, this attachment would not go. But, when he acquired the true knowledge - that all is Brahman and the rest are the illusions wrought by Maya, he realised that though he had all the Punya, unless he donated a bull his merit world not be as much as to offer him a nook in the Vaikuntha, the Realm of Vishnu.

Concluding both the stories, sage Vashishtha told Dharmavastu : "Remember that no matter how well you behave in this world, unless you donate the bull or unless it is donated by your descendants after your death, your soul would not earn the place in the Vaikuntha. Donating the bull gets you the merit due to a performer of a 100 ashwamedha Yagya. Now you must go to Pushkar and donate the bull."

The king did so and earned his place in heaven.

The main point of the story needs to be clarified. In the Hindu faith, the bull is often compared with Dharma. Donating the bull symbolically means one's spreading the noble virtues of his faith. Hence, the importance of the ceremony called Vrishot sarga.

The whole significance of the post-mortem rites among the

Hindus is to ensure that the soul is given its due, however, even though it may be without the body. The physical bonds may be ephemeral, but they have their importance. This Garuda Purana emphasises this point that the person doesn't die even after his death. It leaves the bonds intact till at least four year of his departure from this mortal world.

Ancestors And Their Shraddha

Garuda asked : "Lord Having heard from you all about he Preta-karma (the last rites) and the Shraddha, I want to ask : How the ancestors accept the 'pindas'. How do they come? They have no bodies when their Shraddha is performed. Please dispel my confusion. Lord Vishnu said : "At every Shraddha ceremony, the Brahmanas are invited. The ancestors enter the bodies of the Brahmanas and thus partake of the Pindas. The learned say that only one fourth of what is offered actually reaches the ancestors. In this connection, I tell you the story of Rama and Sita."

Rama and Sita had to go to the forest for 14 years to ensure that Dashrath's promise to Kaikeyi was not falsified. Although, he fulfilled his vow, he couldn't survive and died in the separation from Rama.

Rama was in the forest when he learnt about his father's demise. As had been the traditions, the eldest son of the Solar Dynasty had to perform the Shraddha of his father. He asked Sita to prepare the food and several sages were invited on the Shraddha day. But while she had prepared the food, when the sages came to partake of the same, Sita was nowhere to be found. Rama and Lakshman waited for a long time but Sita was not traceable. Finally, they had to serve the food to the invited Brahmanas themselves. When the guests had left, Sita appeared.

"Where were you?" Rama asked rather sternly.

"I was hiding," replied Sita. "I was ashamed to appear before the guests." "Ashamed of what?" asked Rama rather angrily, "What was there to be ashamed of?"

"Well", Sita began to say: "I saw your father, grandfather and great grandfather sitting down to eat with the other guests. How could have I appeared before them in these thin clothes that I am wearing. I was also ashamed to offer the honoured guests such poor food. That is why I hid myself is shame and waited until they had left." Concluding the story, Lord Vishnu told Garuda that "this way the ancestors do come symbolically

88

at their ceremonies. Hence the guests (the invited Brahmanas) must be treated as honourably as though they are your living ancestors."

Then Garuda asked: "When the ghosts are without body, how do they manage to pester people. How are the accursed souls are able to escape from hell?

"In the same manner that prisoners escape from the prisons. Ghosts are incapable of damaging anybody physically. But what they do is that they enter into the brains of the weak and the gullible and thus make them damage themselves. They would force them behave in a wrong way, so as to make their bodies sick. These ghosts may be available only in Kaliyug. There have never been any ghosts in the earlier ages. The ghosts exploit one's guilty conscience."

Garuda, "How does one know that the ghosts are around?"

"The signs are fairly obvious," replied Vishnu. "Animals die and friends fight. The children turn against their parents. There may be an outbreak of fire without any apparent reason. There are all sorts of happening of unpleasant events."

"What should one do to get rid of these disturbances," Garuda asked.

"Perform the Shraddha ceremony for the evil spirits. Feeding Brahmanas, donating alms to the temple and fulfilling the needy persons' wants as best as one can are some of the ways to pacify the evil spirits. Chanting Gayatri Mantra and performing a Yagya or a havan ensures their early redemption. Among the ghost the most deadly is a pishaacha'. If it is known that such a ghost is around, the first thing that is to be done is to bathe in a teertha. A bilwa (wood-apple) tree should be watered next. And finally the learned, deserving Brahmans should be given grain. Their chanting the Gayatri Mantra would rescue one even from the deadliest 'Pishaada."

"Remember that a man serves his own interest best when he does three things.

1. Remain kind to all beings.
2. Keeps control over his senses
3. Believes that all beings have to perish one day.

He who doesn't believe in the certitude of death and commits foul deeds is like the useless udder which keeps hanging from a she-goat's neck. He who is kind, looks after all with his best intentions and feeds the needy, escapes most of the sins. Although the best donation is gifting away a milch cow, the following donation must be made to ensure a peaceful living in this life and in the next as well.

1. Kanyadaan (donating one's daughter to a deserving groom)

2. Vishotsarga (donating the bull)

3. Making a donation at the teerthas with a definite resolve.

4. Donating one's blood for other's health.

Apart from there, one should also have the wells and ponds made, parks and gardens laid out and noble hermits kept well fed. These acts take away all the blemishes that may have clouded one's righteous vision. Man should realise that these acts form the eternal duty of a man. These acts not only improve one's life on the earth, but also help him get a good status after death in Yama's realm." Further, dwelling on the moral duties of man, Lord Vishnu said : "In Satyayug, the righteous conduct or the Dharma stands on all the four pillars called Satya, Gyan, Tapa and Daya, [truth, knowledge, devotion to one's objective and compassion for all.] But in the Treta, only Satya, Gyan and Daya remain. In Dwapar, only two Gyan and Daya remain. While in Kaliyug the sole support of Dharma remains only in Daya or compassion".

Then the Lord dwelt upon the vices that Kaliyug would be replete with. In that age, the best way to stay on the righteous path, concluded Soota ji, is to remember Lord Vishnu's name for this is the only boat that doesn't sink in the tempestuous ocean, called Kaliyug.

Epilogue

Garuda Purana is a Sathrika Purana and bracketed with Vishnu, Narada, Bhagwat, Padma and Varah Purana. It has now 19000 shlokas available. It is divided in two parts. The Poorva Khanda and the Uttar Khanda.

It is one of the most significant Puranas for the devout, because it is the only Purana which gives a graphic description of the soul's journey after the death of the body. That is the reason why it is generally recited among the traditional Hindu family in the immediate aftermath of a death occurring in the family. It also gives a sense of logic to most of the post-mortem ceremonies adhered to by the Hindu faith. Of course, the description are quite hair-raising at times when the Purana gives the details about the hells one has to live in as the consequence of a given vile deed, it indirectly acts as a deterrent factor for those who listen to it. Even though nothing conclusive can be proved about the events that occur after one's death in the astral world, this Purana, narrated in the question -answer session between Garuda and Lord Vishnu, does appear to be somewhat based on logic. Isn't it natural for the stealer of the food to be totally starved in the next birth? In fact, most of the punishments declared by this Purana give a brief glimpse of a sound divine jurisprudence!

The Purana concludes with Garuda, having obtained answers to all his questions, touches Lord Vishnu's feet and expresses his gratefulness to the Lord for having imparted to him the most secret knowledge about a soul's journey after its exit from the body.

He then goes to sage Kashyapa and conveys this knowledge to him. Since Garuda was the first to spread this knowledge it came to be known as Garuda Purana. The knowledge of this sacred text then percolated down to the sages-from Kashyapa to Bhrigu to Vashishtha. Vashishtha narrated it to Vamadeva who passed it on to Parashar. From Parashar it came to sage Vedavyas who made Romaharshan compile it.

It was from Romaharshan a also called Soota ji - that this knowledge reached the whole assembly of the sages in the holy spot of Nemisharnya.

Concluding the recital, he said : "I have recited for you all that I had learnt. The person who reads this Purana or hears its recital is sure to get much happiness in this world as well as in the next. This sacred text gives men true knowledge. Let us now thank Vedavyas for having allowed us to be enlightened with this most rare knowledge.

All the sages were delighted. They not only thanked Vedavyas mentally but also Romaharshan, repeatedly saying : "Blessed are you! Indeed we are also blessed to have you amidst us to enlighten us this way.'

Great Punya is acquired from reading or hearing the Garuda Purana. But its reciter must be given some alms. Else no Punya (merit) will be accrued to one. In case nothing could be given, then at least the 1000 names of Vishnu should be chanted orally or mentally.

---

1. Given ahead.

Thousand Names of Lord Vishnu

Lord Vishnu's thousand names or 'Vishnusahastranam' has great significance for a devotee of the Lord Bheeshma, the legendary Grand uncle of the Kaurav and the Pandavas. While instructing Yudhisthir before he quit his mortal frame, he says in the 'Mahabharat' that chanting the thousand names of Lord Vishnu is the most effective Incantation or Mantra to ensure all kinds of happiness, pleasure and bliss to the chanter by the Grace of Lord Vishnu, not only in this world, but also in the next. For the benefit of the curious reader, the brief meaning of these names has also been given alongside.

1: Vishwam: The cause of the happening of the world.

2: Vishnu: All pervading.

3: Vashatkār: The object of the Vashat worship in the Yagya.

4: Bhootabhavya bhavatprabhu: Master of the past, present and future.

5: Bhootakrita: The creator of the physical World.

6: Bhootabhrita: The Sustainer of the world (physical).

7: Bhāvah: Eternal and Self-created.

8: Bhootātma: The Dwelling spirit in every being's soul.

9: Bhootabhāvan. The Creator and Sustainer of the Physical World.

10: Pootātma: The soul Purified.

11: Paramātma: The Supreme Spirit.

12: Muktānām Paramā : Gatih The ulitimate stage of the Liberated Soul.

13: Avyayah: Imperishable.

14: Purushah: Dweller in the Pur (body).

15: Sakshee: Witness to all happenings.

16: Kshetragya: He who knows all about the body and its nature.

17: Akshārah: Undecayable.

18:	Yogah:	The summit combination of mind and body.
19:	Yogavidām Neta:	The leader Who Knows Yoga.
20:	Pradhān purusheshwar:	The Master of Nature and Being.
21:	Nārasim havapuh:	Man-Iion bodied.
22:	Shreemān:	He who holds Lakshmi close to his bosom.
23:	Keshava:	Symbolising the Trinity with Brahma representing(Ka), Vishnu(ā), Mahadeva (Ish).
24:	Purushottam:	The Best Among the Decayable and Undecayble bodies.
25:	Sarvah:	All in All.
26:	Sharvah:	The Destroyer of the Creation (at Dissolution).
27:	Shivah:	The Auspicious Form, beyond the three Attributes.
28:	Sthānu:	Stable.
29:	Bhootadi:	The root cause of all beings.
30:	Nidhirvyayah:	The Imperishable embodiment of the bodily form surving through the Dissolution.
31:	Sambhavah:	Emerging at will.
32:	Bhāvanah:	The Bestower of Fruit of Actions.
33:	Bharta:	The Sustainer of the World, who gives food etc. to Beings.
34:	Prabhavah:	The Special (Divine) Existence.
35:	Prabuh:	The Lord of All.
36:	Ishwar:	The Lord of All Opulence.
37:	Swayambhoo:	The Self-Created Lord.
38:	Shambhuh:	The Bestower of Bliss to the Devotees.
39:	Āditya:	The son of mother Aditi.
40:	Pushkarāksha:	The Lotus Eyed.
41:	Mahāswanah:	One who is beyond life and death.
43:	Dhātā:	The Carrier of All.
44:	Vidhātā:	The Creator of deeds and their fruits.
45:	Dhaturuttamah:	The Creator of the best deeds and their effect.
46:	Aprameyah:	Not Proveable by evidence etc.
47:	Hrisheekeshah:	The Master of Senses.

48:	Padmanābhah:	Having lotus in the Navel from which originated Creation.
49:	Amaraprabhu:	The Master of the celestials.
50:	Vishwakarma:	The Creator of the whole world.
51:	Manuha:	The progenitor.
52:	Twashta:	The Cause of decay in all beings at the time of Pralaya or Dissolution.
53:	Sthavishtha:	Huge-bodied.
54:	Sthaviro Dhruvah:	Very Ancient and Very Stable.
55:	Agrihāhya:	Incomprehensible fully by mind.
56:	Stāshwatah:	Eternal.
57:	Krishnah:	Drawing everyone's attention forcibly by his Extreme Beauty: Lord Krishna.
58:	Lohitaksha:	The Red-Eyed.
59:	Pratardanah:	Destroyer of Beings at the time of Dis-solution.
60:	Prabhootah:	Well endowed with knowledge, opulence and virtues.
61:	Trikakbhh dadhām:	The Support of Top, Middle and Bottom Quarters (Directions).
62.	Pavitram.	All purifie.
63:	Mangalam param:	Supremely Auspicious.
64:	Ishaanah:	The Controller of all Spirits.
65:	Prānadah:	The Giver of life.
66:	Jyeshtha:	The Eldest (among all).
67:	Shreshtha:	The Best.
68:	Prajāpati:	The Sustainer of All Being; the progenitor.
69:	Hiranyagarbha:	Permeating like life in the primal Aurum Ovam.
70:	Pranah:	Life-force of every being.
71:	Bhoogarbhah:	The Sustainer of Earth in its Embryonic stage.
72:	Mādhavah:	The Master of Goddess Lakshmi.
73:	Madhusoodanah:	The Slayer of the Demon Madhu.
74:	Ishah:	Omnipotent Lord.
75:	Vikrami:	Chivalrous.
76:	Dhanvi:	Wielder of the Bow Sharnga.
77:	Medhāvee:	Precocious.
78:	Vikramah:	The Order-Setter
80:	Anuttamah:	Peerless.

81:	Durādharsha:	Unassailable.
82:	Kritagya:	Grateful {who reqards greatly for even very little effort in his worship}.
83:	Kritiha:	The Motivating force in the Being's Efforts.
84:	Atmavān:	Reposed in His Own Glory. {The Konwer of self}.
85:	Sureshah:	The Lord of the gods.
86:	Sharanam:	The Shelter of All.
87:	Sharm:	The form of the Supreme Being.
88:	Vishwareta:	The cause of the World.
89:	Prajābhavah:	The Progenitor of All Beings.
90:	Ahah:	The Light-form.
91:	Samvatsarah:	The Setter of Time-Cycle.
92:	Vyālah:	He-like a Serpent-no body could hold Him.
93:	Pratyaya:	Comprehensible only to the Best Brain.
94:	Sarvadarshanah:	The Seer of All.
95:	Adah:	Beginning Less.
96:	Sarveshwarah:	The God of all gods.
97:	Siddha:	Ever evident.
98:	Siddhi:	The Net Result of All.
99:	Sarvādih:	The root cause of all beings.
100:	Acchyuta:	Infallible.
101:	Vrishākapi:	Like the Bull and Monkey or the Dharma and its tenets; also like the Bull and Boar.
102:	Ameyātma:	Indefinable Body.
103:	Sarvayogavinihstratah:	Comprehensible by scores of means, ordained by the Scriptures.
104:	Vasuh:	The Abode of All Beings.
105:	Vasumanah:	Large Hearted.
106:	Satyah:	The Truth.
107:	Samātma:	The Spirt Dwelling Evenly Among All Beings.
108:	Asammitah:	Immeasurable.
109:	Samah:	Equinamous.
110:	Amogh:	Unerring.
111:	Pundereekakhshah:	The One Having Lotus Like eyes.

112: Vrishakarma:	The Doer of the Deeds to Sustain Dharma.
113: Vrishākriti:	The Bull-like form (of Dharma).
114: Rudrah:	He who Removes the cause of Sorrow.
115: Bahushira:	The One with Many Heads.
116: Babhruha:	The Nourisher of the Realms.
117: Vishwayoni:	The Origin of the World.
118: Shuchishrava:	The one with Noble Glory.
119: Amritah:	Immortal.
120: Shāshwat-sthanu:	Ever lasting and Stable.
121: Varāroha:	The High Rider.
122: Mahātāpah:	Manifestative form (result) of the Great penance.
123: Sarvagah:	The All-pervading Cause.
124: Sarvavidbhanu:	The All-Konwing Enlightenment.
125: Visvaksenah:	The Pulveriser of the Demonic forces merely by the preparation to fight.
126: Janardanah:	The Destroyer of peoples' (devotees) distress.
127: Vedah:	The Manifested learinng-the veda-form.
128: Vedavita:	One who knows the real meaming of the Vedas.
129: Avyangah:	Perfect in every sense, or He who has nothing that is imperfect.
130: Vedangah:	Who has vedas as His Body Parts (i.e; the ultimate fount of Knowledge).
131: Vedagya:	The knower of the Vedas.
132: Kavi:	The poet (Knowing every thing).
133: Lokadhyaksha:	Master of All Realms.
134: Surādhyaksha:	The Head of gods.
135: Dharmādhyaksha:	The Head of the Dharma; the one who decides what is Dharma and Adharma or what is noble and What is iniquitous.
136: Kitākrita:	He who does action without cause.
137: Chaturātma:	The spirit of the four pronged world.

138:Chaturvyooha	The four arrays of life: Creation, sustenance, destruction and survival.
139:Chaturbhuja:	The four Armed (Lord Vishnu).
140:Chaturandrishta:	The four-jawed form (of Lord Narasimha).
141:Bhrajishnu:	Uniformly radiant form.
142:Bhojanam:	The nourishment (Provider to the devotees).
143: Bhokta:	The Sufferer in the form of Porush (Being) of punishment and Enjoyer of the rewards.
144:Sahishnu:	Tolerant.
145:Jagadādijah:	self-originating Primal Aurum ovam-the root of the world.
146:Anaghah:	The Sinless.
147:Vijaya:	The Excellor in all matches.
148:Jeta:	A Natural Victor.
149:Vishwayoni:	The Procreator of the world.
150:Punarvasu:	The Spirit which repeatedly comes back to the body.
151:Upendra:	The younger brother of Indra.
152:Vāman:	Incarmating Vāman (the Dwarf).
153:Pranshu:	Growing very high to jump across all the three realms.
154:Amogha:	One Who does not make futile attempts.
155:Shuchi:	The Purifier (to all by his worship).
156:Urjita:	Supermely Energised.
157:Ateendra:	Excelling over Indra in the self-knowledge.
158:Sangrah:	One who collects everything at the time of Dissolution (Pralaya).
159:Sargah:	The Cause of the Creation.
160:Dhritātma:	Beyond the cycle of life and death, the one who creates Himself at will.
161:Niyamah:	The One Who Brings Ordar in Creator.
162:Yamah:	The Controlling Deity Inside every being.

163:Vedya:	Approachable by those who seek their welfare.	
164:Vaidya:	Well versed in all Knowledge.	
165:Sadayogi:	Ever reposing in the yoga.	
166:Veerahā:	Slayer of the demons for protecting Dharma.	
167:Mādhava:	The Lord of All Konwledge.	
168:Madhu:	The Delighter of every heart like nectar.	
169:Ateendriya:	Beyond the approach of senses.	
170:Mahamayah:	The Great Illusor.	
171:Mahotsāha:	Ever enthusiastic to create, sustain and Dissolute the world.	
172:Mahābalah:	Supremely Powerful.	
173:Mahābuddhi:	Supremely Wise.	
174:Mahāveerya:	Supremely Valorous.	
175:Mahāshakti:	Supremely Competent.	
176:Mahadyuti:	Supremely Radiant.	
177:Anirdeshyavapu:	Of Undefineable Image.	
178:Mahdridhrika:	He who supported the mount Madar at the time of churning the ocean for getting nectar as also the Govardhan (in His Krishnā Form) for protection of cows.	
179:Maheshvāsa:	Weilder of a Great Bow.	
180:Maheebharta:	The Giver of food to earth.	
181:Sreeman:	One endowed with oppulence	
182:Ameyatma:	Immeasurable Being	
183:Shreeniwas:	The Abode of Lakshmi.	
184:Satāngati:	The final Refuge of the noble.	
185:Aniruddha:	Indomitable without true devotion.	
186:Surānanda:	The Delighter of gods.	
187:Govindah:	Comprehensible through the Vedas study.	
189:Mareechi:	The Radiance of the radiant.	
190:Daman:	The queller of the delinquence.	
191:Hamsa:	The Swan whom He Created to enlighten Brahma.	
192:Suparna:	Master of Garuda who has beautiful wing.	
193:Bhujagottam:	The best among the serpents, Sheshanag.	

194:Hiranyanabha:	One having aureate navel for the creation of the world.
195:Sutapah:	On who performs right penances.
196:Padmānabh:	One having a lotus in His navel.
197:Prajāpati:	Lord of all creation.
198:Amrityu:	The One Without Death.
199:Sarvadrika:	One who sees all.
200:Sinha:	Destroyer of the wicked.
201:Sandhātā:	One who brings efforts and rewards together.
202:Sandhimān:	One who fills the gap between the effor and the result.
203:Sthir:	Immutable.
204:Aja:	One who cleanses His devotees' heart from vices.
205:Durmarshan:	Whose (dazzling) radiance is unbearable.
206:Shasta:	Ruler over all.
207:Vishrutātmā:	Renowned in the Scriptures.
208:Surāriha:	Slayer of the gods'enemies.
209:Guru:	Teacher of all.
210:Gurutam:	The Greatest Teachar.
211:Dhām:	The final refuge of all.
212:Satya:	True Being.
213:Satya Parākram:	One who performs real feats.
214:Nimisha:	Whose eyers are closed in the yoga-meditation.
215:Animish:	Who Incarnated in the fish form.
216:Sragvee:	One who dons Vaijayanti garland.
217:Vāchaspati: Rudāradhee	The Master of All Knowledge that reveals the Reality.
218:Agranee:	Who Moves in the Vanguard (and take the aspirant to final release).
219:Grāmani:	Leader of a group.
220:Shreemān:	One with all glory and opulence.
221:Nyayah:	The argument in logic proved by facts.
222:Neta:	The Driver (of the world in the form of a vehicle)
223:Sameeran:	Permeating the whole world like air.
224:Sahastra moordhā:	A Thousand headed.
225:Sahastrāksha:	A Thousand Eyed.

100

226: Vishwatma:	The spirit of the world.
227: Sahastrapādā:	One with thousand feet.
228: Āvartan:	One who keeps this global cycle moving.
229: Nivrittātma:	The Released Soul.
230: Samvrat:	Enveloped by His own Illusion
231: Sampramardan:	Crushing every one is His Rudra form.
232: Ahahsamvartak:	One who begins the day or year (in the form of the sun).
233: Vahni:	The fire which accepts all offering (in a sacrifice).
234: Anilah:	The wind in the form of vital air.
235: Dharanidhar:	Supporter of the Earth (In the form of the Boar and the Serpent).
236: Suprasād:	Gracious to even the wicked (by granting space in His Abode after slaying their bodies).
237: Prasannātma:	The Delighted soul.
238: Vishwadhrik:	The Support of the World.
239: Vishwabhuk:	The Nourisher of the world.
240: Vibhuha:	All Pervading.
241: Satkartā:	Hospitable to His devotees.
242: Satkrita:	Adorable by those worshipped.
243: Sādhu:	One who Make the Devotees achieve their aim.
244: Jahnu:	One who destroys beings at the time of Dissolution.
245: Nārāyanah:	One who reposes in water, Or, Water is whose home, or Abode.
246: Narah:	One who guides the noble.
247: Asankheya:	He who can't be represented by figures.
248: Aprameyaatmā:	Immeasurable by any scale.
249: Vishistah:	Especial, exquisite.
250: Shistakrita:	Who controls all.
251: Shuchi:	Supremely pious.
252: Siddhartha:	He who has succeded in his mission.
253: Siddhasankalpah:	One with resolute determination.
254: Siddhidah:	Bestower rewards according to the doers efforts.

255:Siddhi sādhan:	He who provides means for accomplishment.
256:Vrishāhi:	Reposing the effects of the sacrifice (Yagya) like Dwadasha and others within his control.
257:Vrishabhah:	One who showers choicest gifts for his devotees.
258:Vishnuh:	Embodiment of nobility.
259:Vrishaparva:	The stairs of Dharma to seek salvation for the aspirants.
260:Vrishodar:	Holding the Dharma close to heart.
261:Vardhan:	One who ensures prosperity to His devotees.
262:Vivaktah:	One who remains aloof from the world.
263:Shrutisagar:	An ocean of Vedic knowledge.
264:Subhujah:	Of well formed arms (for protecting the world).
265:Durdharah:	He who can't be supported by anyone.
266:Vardhaman:	He who grows life in the world.
267:Vāgmi:	The originator of the Vedic speech.
268:Mahendra:	Lord of Lords.
269:Vasudah:	Bestower of wealth.
270:Vasuh:	The Embodiment of riches.
271:Naikaroopah:	In Myriad forms.
272:Vrihadroopah:	The Universal form.
273:Shipavishtah:	The Radiance in the sun rays.
274:Prakāshan:	One who Illumines everything.
275:Ojastejodyutidhar:	One who has vitality, shine and radiance.
276:Prakāshatma:	The Enlightened Soul.
277:Pratapan:	Providing Heat to all luminaries like sun and fire.
278:Riddha:	Well versed in Dharma, Knowledge etc.
279:Spashtākshar:	With well defined letter (word) like 'AUM'.
280:Mantra:	Comprehended by hymns of Rig, Sām and Yajur vedas.
281:Chandrānshu:	Like cool moonlight to the nobles distrersed with mundane heat.

282:Bhaskardyuti:	Radiant like the sun.
283:Amritānshoodbhava:	The origin of the moon, the sea, at the time of churning.
284:Bhanuh:	He who gives light to see.
285:Shashbindu:	Like the moon-with the rabbit sign in the heart-to rear up the world.
286:Sureshwar:	Lord of the gods.
287:Aushadhim:	The Medicine to cure all worldly ills.
288:Jagatah-Setu:	The bridge to go across this world.
289:Satyadharma parat : kramah	The Manifestation of the strength of Truth and Dharma.
290:Bhootabhavya : bhavannath	The Lord the past, present and future of all beings.
291:Pavanh:	Moving like fast wind.
292:Pāvanah:	Purifying by His very look.
293:Analah:	(In the form of) Fire.
294:Kāmha:	Destroyer of the sense of doership in his devotes.
295:Kāmkrita:	Granter of His devotees wishes.
296:Kantah:	Extremely beautiful.
297:Kāma:	The Trinity (with 'ka' representing Brahma,'a'representing Vishnu and 'ma' representing Mahadeva or Shiv).
298:Kāmpradah:	Bestower to his devotees their desired objects.
299:Prabhu:	Omnipotent Almighty.
300:Yugādikrita:	Harbinger of the beginning of an epoch.
301:Yugāvarta:	He who rotates all the four yugas in order like His Chakra (discus).
302:Naikamaya:	Creator of Many Illusions.
303:Mahāshana:	He who devours everything at the end of an epoch.
304:Adrishya:	Invisible (for those infatuated with sensual objects).
305:Vyaktaroopa:	Manifest for (of Divinity).
306:Sahastrajit:	Vanquisher of a thousand foes.
307:Anantajit:	Vanquisher of a thousand foes.
308:Ishta:	The Chosen Divinity.

309:Avishishta:	The best even without any description of the qualities.
310:Shishteshtah:	The Chosen God of the noble.
311:Shikhandi:	Making peacock feather His head ornament (in the Krishna form).
312:Nahushah:	Who enchants the mortals by his illusions.
313:Vrasha:	He who fulfils all desires.
314:Krodhahā:	Destroyer of the anger.
315:Krodhakritkarta:	Showing His wrath upon the wicked to reform them.
316:Vishwabāhu:	Having arms in every direction.
317:Maheedharah:	The support of the World.
318:Achyuta:	Free from all the six vile feelings.
319:Prathitah:	Initiator of the process of creaton.
320:Prāna:	The Vital force.
321:Prānadah:	Bestower of life.
322:Vāsavānujah:	Younger brother of Indra.
323:Apānnidhi:	A deep pit like ocean to collect water.
324:Adhishthānam:	The very support of all mortal beings.
325:Apramātah:	Not stingy in granting due reward to his devotee.
326:Pratishthita:	Well established in His Own Glory.
327:Skanda:	Commander of the gods, forces (in this form).
328:Skandadharah:	Upholder of righteousness.
329:Dhurya:	The axis of all movement in the world.
330:Varadah:	Bestower of the desired boon.
331:Vayuvāhan:	The carrier of the wind.
332:Vāsudeva:	The Abode of a all beings.
333:Vrihadbhnu:	The Mighty sun.
334:Ādideva:	Primal Deity.
335:Purandar:	Destroyer of the Cities of demons.
336:Ashoka:	One who rids all of sorrow.
337:Tāran:	One who takes across (the ocean of mundane existence).
338:Tarah:	Who destroys the fright for death and decay.
339:Shoor:	Valiant.

340:Shauri:	Son of chivalrous Vasudeva (In Krishna's form).
341:Janeshwar:	Lord of all beings.
342:Anukool:	Towards our side.
343:Shātāvartā:	Coming in hundred rotations (i.e.incarnating many times to protect Dharma).
344:Padmi:	Wielder of lotus in his hand.
345:Padmanibhekshan:	Having a sight as soft as the stalk of lotus.
346:Padmanābha:	Having a lotus in whose navel region.
347:Arvindākasha:	Having lotus like eyes.
348:Padmagarbha:	Worth concentrating in the lotus of heart.
349:Shareerabhrita:	Nourishing everybody with food.
350:Mahardhi:	Having great glory.
351:Riddha:	Exclling in all match.
352:Vriddhātma:	The ancient soul.
353:Mahāksha:	The Wide Eyed.
354:Garudadhwajā:	He who has Garuda Mark in His Flag.
355:Atul:	Incomparable.
356:Sharabh:	Illumining bodies in orderly manner.
357:Bheema:	Terrible.
358:Samayagya:	The even reward of all the sacrifices.
359:Havirharih:	The Reminder of His share in the Yagya offering and destroyer of sins.
360:Sarvalakshan : lakshanya	Having all comely features.
361:Lagahmivān:	Ever with riches (or Goddess Lakshmi).
362:Samitinjayah	Victor in every war.
363:Vikshar:	Decayless
364:Rohit:	Incarnating in the form of the fish.
365:Margah:	The path to Salvation.
366:Hetu:	The purpose of the world.
367:Damodar:	He whose stomach was tied with a rope (By Yashoda in his Krishna incarnation).

368: Sah:	Tolerating every affliction for the benefit of his devotees.
369: Maheedhar:	The Support of the world.
370: Mahābhāg:	Supremely fortunate.
371: Vegavān:	Very fast moving.
372: Amitāshan:	One who devours the world.
373: Udbhava:	The cause of world's growth or emergence.
374: Kshobhan:	One who agitates Being and Nature before Creation.
375: Deva:	The Deity.
376: Shree garbha:	Preserving every wealth of world inside His stomach.(at the time fo Dissolution).
377: Parmeshwarah:	Supreme Lord, Almighty.
378: Kāranam:	The greatest means of creation.
379: Karanam:	The Prime Cause of World's existence.
380: Karta:	One who is totally free to act.
381: Vikarta:	The special Creator of the realms.
382: Gahan:	Intense and Mysterious.
383: Guhah:	Covering Himself with His Illusive Veil.
384: Vyavasāya:	The very source of Knowledge.
385: Vyavasthān:	One who ordains order in the Creation.
386: Sansthan:	The Abode of Dissolution.
387: Sthānadah:	He Who Granted Firm position (to His Devotees liks Dhruva and Prahlaad).
388: Dhruva:	Indestructible.
389: Parardhi:	One with Great Glory.
390: Paramspashta:	Crystal clear(before his know-ledgeable and discerning devotees).
391: Tushta:	Fully Satiate(God).
392: Pushta:	Fully Healthy.
393: Shubhekshana:	He who ensures welfare merely by His Darshan.
394: Rām:	One Who is Instinct in every bit of Creation.
395: Virām:	The final Resting Place of all beings.

396: Virat:	Indifferent (totally devoid of passion and dullness).
397: Marg:	The ultimate Path of Salvation.
398: Neyah:	Comprehensible by superior Knowledge.
399: Nayah:	The controlling and regulating factor of the world order.
400: Anayah:	Totally free, liberated.
401: Veer:	Brave.
402: Shaktimatan Shreshta:	Mightier than the mightiest.
403: Dharmah:	The Dharma or the conduct of living.
404: Dharma Viduttam:	He who knows the Dharma best.
405: Vaikuntha:	The final Abode of all aspirants.
406: Purusha:	The Primal Person.
407: Prān:	The Vital air.
408: Pranad:	The Giver of Life.
409: Pranav:	The Special form of the Monosyllable 'Om'.
410: Prathu:	Spreading in large billows.
411: Hiranyagarbha:	Holding (in His belly) the Golden Ovam.
412: Shatrughna:	The Slayer of the enemies.
413: Vyāpta:	All round spreading.
414: Vāyu:	The Vital air.
415: Adhokshaja:	Of undecayable form.
416: Ritu:	Visible by the cycle fo time (the seasons).
417: Sudershan:	Having auspicious appearance; good to look at.
418: Kaal:	The Measure of All.
419: Parameshthee:	Excelling in His great glory.
420: Parigriha:	Approachable form all sides by the shelter seekers.
421: Ugra:	The Wrathful, causing fear even in the fire and son gods.
422: Sanvatsarah:	The Beginner of the cycle.
423: Daksha:	Dextrous in all works.
424: Vishrām:	The final Resting Place of all the seekers of Moksha.
425: Vishwadakshin:	The receiver of all 'Dakshina' in the sacrifice arranged by Bali.
426: Vistar:	The cause of expansion of the Universe.

427:Sthāvarathānu:	Though Himself stable yet keeping the world amove.
428:Pramānam:	The ultimate evidence of existence of world.
429:Beejamavyam:	The Imperishable Entity of the world.
430:Artha:	Adorable by all owing to His being bestower of happiness.
431:Anartha:	Having no desire, so it is meaningless to offer Him anything.
432:Māhākoshā:	One with Great Treasure.
433:Mahabhoga:	The Great Enjoyer.
434:Mahadhana:	Supremely and Really Rich.
435:Anirviana:	Free form the surfeit or boredom.
436:Sthavishtha:	Reposing Everywhere.
437:Abhoo:	Unborn.
438:Dharma Yoop:	The pillar of Dharma.
439:Mahāmakha:	Making great a sacrifice (in which offering is made to Him).
440:Nakshatranemi:	The Centre of all planet and constella tions.
441:Nakshatri:	Moon-like.
442:Kshamah:	Competent.
443:Kshāmah:	Capable of quelling all disorders.
444:Sameehanah:	Making conscious efforts for creation.
445:Yagya:	Embodiment of all sacrifices.
446:Ijyah:	Adorable.
447:Mahejyah:	Most Adorable (among all deities).
448:Kratuh:	Lord of the Sacrifice with all the appur tneances.
449:Satram:	Protector of the noble.
450:Satam Gatih:	The ultimate destination of the nobles.
451:Sarvadarshee:	One who looks at all.
452:Vimuktakāmā:	Free form the mortal desires.
453:Sarvagya:	All knowing.
454:Gyanmuttamam:	The Best Knowledge.
455:Suvratah:	Of noble resolve.
456:Sumukhah:	Of beautiful visage.
457:Sukhadah:	Bestower of happiness to His devotee.

458:Sukshmah:	Very Subtle.
459:Sughoshah:	Having a sweet and deep voice.
460:Suhrita:	Kind to all being without any selfish desire.
461:Manohar:	Enchanting.
462:Jitakrodha:	He who has subdued his anger.
463:Veerbāhu:	Mighty Armed.
464:Vidaranah:	Tearing apart the wicked.
465:Swapan:	He who throws everyone in the stupor during the Dissolution (Pralaya).
466:Swavash:	Self-Dependent.
467:Vyāpi:	All pervading.
468:Naikatmā:	Adpiting various forms in every age according to the need of time.
469:Naikakarmakrita:	Indulging in varous activities (like creation, destruction etc.) for people's welfare.
470:Vatsar:	Ultimate Abode of All.
471:Vatsal:	Very Affectionate to His devotees.
472:Vatsy:	Rearing up the heifer (in Vrindavan as Krishna).
473:Ratnagarbh:	Hiding gems inside his person.
474:Dhaneshwar:	Lord of all riches.
475:Dharmgup:	The Protector of Dharma.
476:Dharmakrita:	Showing by action how to uphold the righteousness.
477:Dharmi:	The base of all Dharmic tenets.
478:Sat:	True (Being).
479:Asat:	The False worldly form.
480:Ksharam:	Causing decay in physical entities or the Decadent.
481:Aksaharam:	Making (things) Imperishable.
482:Avigyātā:	Soul in the body is called 'Vigyātā. That which is distinct from it-the supreme spirt-or Lord Vishnu-is Avigyātā.
483:Sahastrānshu:	Like a sun with thousand rays.
484:Vidhātā:	The special carrier of the whole world.
485:Kritalakshan:	Anointed with noble signs like 'Shree Vatsa'.
486:Gabhastinemi:	Reposed like the sun among the rays.

487:Satvastha:	Omnipresent; knowing truth of every heart.
488:Sinha:	Adopting the Lion (visage) for Prahlaad's cause.
489:Bhootamaheshwar:	Lord of all mortal creation.
490:Ādideva:	The Primal Deity.
491:Mahadeva:	The Grand Deity.
492:Devesha:	Lord of all Deities.
493:Devbhridaguru:	The Guru of the gods who takes special care of them.
494:Uttarah:	The other bang of the ocean of metempsychosis.
495:Gopati:	The Lord and protector of Cows (as Krishna).
496:Gopta:	He who protects and nourishes every being.
497:Gyāngamya:	Comprehensible by knowledge.
498:Purātān:	The Ancient Being.
499:Shareerabhootbhrita:	The nourisher of the five basic elements of the body.
500:Bhokta:	The one who Enjoys Eternal Bliss.
501:Kapeendra:	Lord of Monkeys (or King of Monkeys, Shri Rām).
502:Bhooridakshina:	One Who gives fees to the priests liberally.
503:Somepah:	The Partaker of 'Soma' offered to Him in the yagyas.
504:Amritapah:	He who drings nectar and makes other gods also drink ti.
505:Soma:	The moon who nourishes all vegetables.
506:Purujit:	Victorious of many battles.
507:Purusattam:	The Best Universal form.
508:Vinaya:	The Punisher of the Wicked.
509:Jaya:	The Victor (or the cause of victory).
510:Satyasandha:	Veridicious.
511:Dashārha:	Appearing in the Dashārha family.
512:Satvatām Pati:	The Leader of Yadavas and the Lord of his devotees.

513:Jeeva:	The Being.
514:Vinayitāsākshi:	He who discerns the humility of his devotees quickly.
515:Mukundah:	The Bestower of Liberation.
516:Amitavikramah:	Immensely competent to bring Revolution.
517:Ambhonidhi:	Huge like sea, the store of water.
518:Anantātmā:	The Soul Infinite.
519:Mahodadhishaya:	He who Reposes in the Grand Ocean even during Pralay-time, agitation and disturbance.
520:Antakah:	Death like to end being's life (at Pralaya).
521:Ajaha:	Free form blemish of getting birth.
522:Maharhah:	Adorable.
523:Swābhāvya:	Owing to the self-evidence of the Existence, the need of whose birth does not arise.
524:Jitamitrah:	Friend of the wicked's enemies (the gods).
525:Pramodanah:	He who Delights merely by remembering Him.
526:Ānada:	Bliss (or the Manifestation of Bliss).
527:Nandanah:	The Delighter of all.
528:Nandah:	Prosperous with all comforts and luxuries.
529:Satyadhrma:	The Truth of the faith.
530:Trivikram:	Measuring three realms in His three steps. (Vāman).
531:Maharshi: Kapilācharya	The Propounder of the Sankhya Theory (the sage Kapil).
532:Kritagya:	Grateful (to his devotees for the devotion).
533:Medanipati:	The Lord of Earth.
534:Tripadah:	He Who measured all the realms in three steps.
535:Tridashādhyaksha:	Lord of all gods, demons and men.
536:Mahashringah:	He Who Has a Great Thorn (as the Boar).

111

537:Kritāntakrita:	He Who Removes the need of the deed when invoked {i.e., He ilberates when worshipped}.
538:Mahāvārah:	The Great Boar.{The Second Incarnation}.
559:Govindah:	He Who is Capable of Reclaiming the sunken earth.
540:Sushenah:	Well attended by an army of lieutenants.
541:Kanakāngadi:	He Who Has a golden armlet.
542:Guhyah:	The Occult {Who occultly resides in every heart}.
543:Gabheerah:	Of very deep nature.
544:Gahan:	Very Intense.
545:Guptah:	Secret, incomprehensible by description.
546:Chakragadadharam:	The Weilder of the Disc and the Mace.
547:Vedhah:	One Who Constitutes Everything.
548:Swāngah:	Self-supporting.
549:Ajitah:	Invincible.
550:Krishnah:	Lord ShriKrishna.
551:Dridhah:	Determined.
552:Sankarshanoachhyut:	Infallible by any attraction.
553:Varuna:	The Lord of Waters.
554:Vārunah:	The son of Lord of waters, varuna-or Vashishth.
555:Vriksha:	The Tree of Ashwattha (The Peepal Tree).
556:Pushkarāksha:	The Lotus Eyed.
557:Mahāmanah:	He Who accomplishes anything by merely thinking about it.
558:Bhagwan:	The God having all the six divine Attributes.
559:Bhagha:	He Who withdraws all opulence of his devotees in order to test the firmess of their devotion.
560:Ānandi	He Who is Manifestation of Bliss.
561:Vanmāli:	He Who Has a garland of wild flowers-Vaijayanti.
562:Halāyudh:	The Plough-Holder (Balrām).
563:Āditya:	Son of Aditi.
564:Jyotirāditya:	The Brilliant Sun.

565:Sahishnu:	Capable of bearing all the opposites'effect simultaneously.
566:Gatisattam:	The noble's destination.
567:Sudhanvā:	Weilder of a beautiful bow.
568:Khanda Parashu:	In the form of Parashurām, the Axe Holder.
569:Dārunah:	Terrible (For those treading unrighteous path).
570:Dravinapradah:	The Bestower of riches to His devotes who want them.
571:Divasprik:	Spreading upto heaven.
572:Savradrigvyās:	The All Seeing Vyas (Vedavyas)
573:Vāchaspatiryonijah:	Master of Knowledge and not born thorugh the vagina (i.e; Self created).
574:Trisāmā:	Whose glory is sung by the three Vedas.
575:Samagah:	He who sings Sām Veda.
576:Nirvānam:	The Abode of the Liberated Soul.
577:Sām:	Embodiment of Sām Veda.
578:Bheshajam:	The Medicine for Mortal ills.
579:Bhishak:	The ultimate Physician to cure all ills.
580:Sanyās-krita:	He who Ordained Sanyas-Ashram for the aspirant desiring salvation.
581:Shamah:	The Queller (of the disturbance caused by the wicked).
582:Shantih:	Embodiment of Quietude.
583:Nishtha:	The Object of everybody's loyalty.
584:Shantih:	Peace personified.
585:Parayanam:	The final Abode of the Salvation seekers.
586:Shubhāngah:	He Who has Beautiful organs and Body.
587:Shantidah:	He Who Gives peace.
588:Srashta:	The Creator.
589:Kumudah:	The Delighter of the Earth.
590:Kuvaleshaya:	He Who Reposes on the Serpent's coil in water.
591:Gohitah:	The well-wisher of cows.
592:Gopati:	Lord of cows.
593:Gopta:	Keeping Himself Enveloped by His Creative Illusion.

594:Vrishabhāksha:	Having Gracious look for all.
595:Vrishabha-priya:	The Lover of Dharma.
596:Anivarti:	The Lover of Dharma.
597:Nivrarti:	Indomitable in War or in the protection of Dharma.
598:Samksheptā:	He Who Condenses the World in a trice.
599:Kshemkrita:	The protector of the shelter-seekers.
600:Shiv:	The Auspicious.
601:Sreevatsavaksha:	Having'Shree vatsa' mark upon His Bosom.
602:Shreevāsah:	The Abode of Lakshmi.
603:Shreepati:	Lord of Lakshmi.
604:Shreematam Varah:	The Best Groom.
605:Shreedah:	Giver of all wealth.
606:Shreesha:	Lord of Lakshmi.
607:Shreeniwas:	Abode of Lakshmi.
608:Shreenidhi:	Fount of all wealth.
609:Shreevibhavan:	Granter of the desired fruit according to devotees'efforts.
610:Shreedhara:	He in whose bosom reposes Lakshmi.
611:Shreekarah:	He Who Gives all opulence and peace to His devotees.
612:Shreyah:	Auspiciousess personified.
613:Shreemān:	Having all sorts of riches.
614:Lokatryashrāya:	The Support for all the three Realms.
615:Swaksha:	Having Beautiful Eyes.
616:Swangah:	Having Beautiful organs.
617:Shatānanda:	Bestower of a Hundred Kinds of Happiness and Bliss.
618:Nandi:	Image of the Supreme Bliss.
619:Jyotirganeshwar:	Lord of all luminaries.
620:Vijitatmā:	He Who Has His Mind under His Control.
621:Avidheyatmā:	Whose real Form is ineffable.
622:Satkirtee:	One with Real Glory.
623:Chinnasamshaya:	He Who Removes All Doubts.
624:Udeerna:	Best Among all Beings.
625:Sarvatashchakshu:	He who can see everything in all directions at all times.

626:Aneesha:	Having no one Above Him.
627:Shāshwatasthira:	Eternal and immutable.
628:Bhooshayah:	He Who slept on the Earth (in the form of Rām).
629:Bhooshanah:	An ornament (of the earth by his incarnations).
630:Bhootih:	The Support of all Existences.
631:Vishokah:	Free from all woes.
632:Shokanāshanah:	Destroyer of sorrow.
633:Archishmān:	The Source of brightness of all luminaries.
634:Architah:	Worshipped by all.
635:Kumbha:	The Pitcher (of existence).
636:Vishuddhātmā:	Pure Soul.
637:Vishodhanah:	He who purifies All.
638:Aniruddha:	Unstoppable.
639:Apratirath:	Having no oppisition.
640:Pradyumna:	Indomitable to His adversary.
641:Amitavikrama:	Of Infinite valour.
642:Kalinemihā:	The slayer of the demon Kalinemi.
643:Veer:	Chivalrous.
644:Shauri:	Born in the family of the gallant (Shree Krishna).
645:Shoorjaneshwar:	The Chosen Lord, owing to His powers, for Indra and other gods.
646:Trilokātamā:	The Spirit pervading the Three Realms.
647:Trilokesha:	The Lord of the Three Realms.
648:Keshavah:	Having hair as shiny as the rays of the sun.
649:Keshihā:	Slayer of Keshi.
650:Hari:	He whose mere rememberance causes all sins and affictions to disappear.
651:Kāmdeva:	The Deity who fulfils all desires.
652:Kāmpal:	Satiator of all desires.
653:Kāmi:	He whose desires are ever fulfilled.
654:Kantah:	Very Enchanting person.
655:Kritagamah:	Author of all scriptures.
656:Anirdeshyavapu:	Whose Divine form is ineffable.
657:Vishnu:	The Lord (of the Trinity who preserves the world).

658:Veerah:	Who treads even without moving his feet and having many divine powers.
659:Anantah:	Infinite.
660:Dhananjaya:	Winner of wealth.
661:Brahmanya:	Protector of the Brahman, the noble and of knowledge.
662:Brahmakrita:	Who created order for Brahmans.
663:Brahma:	In the form of Brahmā, the creator.
664:Brahm:	Supreme spirit.
665:Brahmvivardhanah:	Enhancer of the Brahm (or its Manifestation).
666:Brahmavit:	Knower of the Meaning of the Vedas fully.
667:Brahmanah:	Looking at all without prejudice or prediliction.
668:Brahmi:	The Divine spirit permeating all.
669:Brahmagya:	He who knows Brahm (and scriptures etc).
670:Brahmanpriya:	Darling of Brahmans.
671:Mahākrama:	Perfomer of great feats.
672:Mahākarma:	Perfomer of great deeds.
673:Mahātejah:	The Radiance of the Radiant.
674:Mahoraga:	The Great Serpent (Vāsuki).
675:Mahākratu:	Embodiment of a Great Sacrifice.
676:Mahāyajwa:	He Who Performs Great Sacrifice for peoples' welfare.
677:Māhāyagya:	A Great yagya(Deed or Action).
678:Mahāhavi:	The Great offering.
679:Stavya:	Adorable for every one.
680:Stavapriya:	He who gets propitiated by chanting hymns.
681:Strotram:	The Hymn (For singing Lord's glory).
682:Stuti:	The obtect of orisons.
683:Ranapriya:	He Who loves wars.
684:Poornah:	Perfect in every way.
685:Stota:	He Who creates hymns.
686:Pooriyata:	He Who makes His devotee devoid of want.
687:Punya:	The Spirit behind a meritorious deed.

688: Punyakeerti:	Of noble renown.
689: Anāmayah:	Free from any kind of affliction.
690: Manotava:	Traveller with the speed of mind.
691: Teerthakarah:	Creator of All Knowledege and Its Interpreter.
692: Vasuretā:	The Seed of Existence.
693: Vasupradah:	Bestower of all riches.
694: Vāsudeva:	Son of Vasudeva (Shree Krishna).
695: Vāsuprad:	Bestower of Great Wealth in the form of Moksha (or final release).
696: Vasu:	The Abode of All Beings.
697: Vasumana:	The Dweller in All Hearts.
698: Havi:	The Supreme offering (of the Yagya).
699: Sadgati:	The Final Stage of the noble.
700: Satkriti:	The (Performer of the) Noble Deed (to perserve the world).
701: Sattā:	The Authority
702: Sadbhooti:	Visible in many Forms.
703: Satpāryān:	The Desired Destination of the noble.
704: Shoorsena:	The Commander of the army of Valiants (in His Rām Incarnation, Having Hanumān, Jambvant and others).
705: Yadushrestha:	The Best among the family of Yadu (as Krishna).
706: Sannivās:	The Abode of the noble.
707: Suyāmunah:	Whose Presence conesecrated the river Yamuna bank. (Shree Krishnu).
708: Bhootavās:	The ultimate Abode of all mortals.
709: Vāsudeva:	The Deity who Envelops the world by His Illusion.
710: Sarvāsunilaya:	The Besutiful Home for the noble.
711: Analah:	Endowed with Immense power and wealth.
712: Darpahā:	Browbeater of the arrogant.
713: Driptah:	Immersed in the Eternal Bliss.
714: Durdharah:	Difficul place in heart.
715: Darpadah:	Bestower of the glory to His devotees.
716: Aparājita:	Invincible.

717:Vishwamoorti:	The Form Universal.
718:Mahamoorti:	Of the Grand Image.
719:Deeptimoorti:	Having radiant Image.
720:Amoortimān:	He Whose Image Can't be Defined.
721:Anekamoorti:	Having Myriad Images.
722:Avyaktā:	Unmanifest.
723:Shatmoorti:	Having hundreds of Images.
724:Shatānanah:	Having hundred of faces.
725:Ekah:	Unique.
726:Naikah:	Owing to Many Forms, He is multi-Faceted.
727:Savah:	The Receptacle which holds the sap of the herb soma.
728:Kah:	The Embodiment of Bliss.
729:Kim:	Who Is He-the question.
730:Yat:	Self-Evident.
731:Tat:	The Expander.
732:Padamanuttamam:	The Highest State (aspired by the nobles).
734:Lokanath:	Master of the people.
735:Madhavah:	Born in Madhu's family.
736:Bhaktavatsal:	Kind to His Devotees.
737:Suvarnavarna:	Having Aureate Body Hue.
738:Hemāng:	Having Golden Body (or organs)
739:Varānga:	Having an Exalted physique.
740:Chandanāngadi:	Having His Body anointed with sandal paste.
741:Veeraha:	Slayer of demons for protecting Dharma.
742:Visham:	The only One (Having none like Him).
743:Shoonya:	Beyond all definitons.
744:Dhritāshi:	Resolute with Soft Kindness to His votaries.
745:Achala:	Unmoving (Form His Resolve).
746:Chala:	Moveable (like wind everywhere).
747:Amāni:	Not Caring For His Individual Honour.
748:Manadah:	Bestowing honour (to His devotees).
749:Lokaswami:	Master of all realms.
750:Manya:	Respectable for everyone.

751:Trilokdhrik:	The Lone Support for the Three worlds (heaven, earth and patal).
752:Sumedha:	Having Noble Brilliance.
753:Medhajah:	He who Manlests Himself though Yagya.
754:Dhanya:	The Blessed Lord.
755:Satyamedhā:	Having only Truth carying wisdom.
756:Dharādhar:	The Support of the Earth.
757:Tejovrasha:	He who Showers Brilliance upon His Devotees.
758:Dyutidhar:	Bedight with a Dazzling Brilliance.
759:Sarvashastrabhritām: Narah	The Best Among all the weapon weilders.
760:Pragraha:	He who Accepts offerings of His Devotees.
761:Nigraha:	All Restraint Personified.
762:Vyagrah:	Restless to Fulfil His devotees desires.
763:Naikashringa:	Having many media for His Resounding word.
764:Gadāgrajah:	Elder to Gada.
765:Chaturmoorti:	The Four Visaged Image.
766:Chaturbahu:	Having four Arms.
767:Chaturvyooha:	Encircled by the four arrays (Generations). 3. Four generations are represented by Vāsudeva, Sankarshan (Balram), Pradyumna and Aniruddha).
768:Chaturgatih:	Manifesting in four forms (Rām, Bharat, Lakshman, Shatrughna).
769:Chaturātmā:	Having four forms of consciouness (Mind, Wisdom, the sense of I'ness and heart).
770:Chaturbhāvah:	The origin of Four wants of the body (Dharma, Artha, Kām, Moksha).
771:Chaturvedavita:	He Who knows the Real Meaning of the four vedas.
772:Ekapat:	He Who Measured the World by His One step.
773:Samāvartā:	He Who Keeps the World Moving with even pace.

774:Nrivattatma: The Relaxed Soul.
775:Durjaya: Difficult to subdue.
776:Duratikrama: He whose order is inviolable.
777:Durlabha: Rare to perceive.
778:Durgama: Inaccessible.
779:Durgah: Difficult to reach.
780:Durāvas: Difficult to hold (in one's heart).
781:Durārihā: Slayer of the Demons who tread the unrighteous path.
782:Shubhangah: Having Beautiful Body.
783:Lokasāranga: He who's the Essence of the world.
784:Sutāntu: Having beautiful bond to bind the world in one body.
785:Tantuvardhan: The Enricher of the Mortal Bonds.
786:Indrakarmā: Performing Indra-like Deeds.
787:Mahākarmā: Performer of Great Deeds.
788:Kritakarmā: He Who Has Done All that was Due.
789:Krtitāgam: The Creator of the Vedas.
790:Udbhava: Incarnating Himself at Will.
791:Sundarah: Beautiful.
792:Sundah: Extremely kind.
793:Ratnanābh: Having Navel As Beautiful as a gem.
794:Sulochana: Of Beautiful Eyes.
795:Arkah: Adorable by the adored.
796:Vājasanah: Bestower of Food to the Hungry.
797:Shringi: Having a Thorn (in his Fish Incannation)
798:Jayantah: The Victor of the enemy.
999:Sarvavijjayee: Victor All.
800:Suvarnabindu: Having Golden pointed Name. 4. In Nagari script, it is written ॐ (the point represents god)] (the word OM).
801:Akshobhya: He who cannot be Disturbed or agitated.
802:Sarvāgeeshwar eshwar: The Lord of all Sounds.
803:Mahahrida: The Great pond (of Bliss for the Yogis).

804:Mahagarta:	The Grand Entity (Undecayed even in the pralaya).
805:Mahabhoota:	The Grand Entity (Undecayed even in the pralaya).
806:Mahanidhi:	The Grand Abode of All.
807:Kumudah:	Redeemer of the Earth ('Ku')'s burden.
808:Kundarah:	Penetrator of the Earth (to kill Hiranyakshapa)
809:Kundah:	The Donor of the Earth (to sage Kashyapa).
810:Purjanya:	He who showers All Desired Objects.
811:Pāvan:	Purifier.
812:Anilah	Ever Awake.
813:Amritānsh:	He whose Hope is Never Belied.
814:Amritavapu:	Of Imperishable Body.
815:Sarvagya:	Omniscient.
816:Sarvatomukh:	Having Face in Every Direction.
817:Sulabha:	Easily Accessible (to the devotee).
818:Suvratah:	He who Eats Good Food (offered by His devotees).
819:Siddhah:	Endowed with perfection
820:Shatrujita:	Vanquisher of the Enemy.
821:Shatrutapān:	Scorcher of the Foe.
822:Nyagrodha:	The Grand Banyan.
823:Udambar:	He who stays Beyond the skies.
824:Chānoorāndhranishoodan:	He who killed the Werstler of Andhra tribe, Chānoora.
825:Ashwatth:	The Peepal (tree-believed to be most pious).
826:Sahastrārchi:	Having Infinite Rays.
827:Saptajivha:	The Seven Tongued Flame.
828:Saptadha:	The Fire with Seven Radiances.
829:Saptavāhan:	The Sun Having vehicle with Seven Horses.
830:Amoortih:	Formless.
831:Anagha:	Free from all sins.
832:Bhayakrita:	Frightening (to the wicked).
833:Achintya:	Beyond Comprehension.
834:Bhayanashan:	Destroyer of the fright (for his devotees).

835:Anuh:	The Molecule.
836:Vribhatah:	Huge.
837:Krishah:	Very light and thin.
838:Sthoola:	The Heavy (Huge)Bodied.
839:Gunabhrita:	The Mine of All virtues.
840:Nirgunah:	The Attributeless.
841:Mahān:	The Great.
842:Adhrita:	Whom no one could carry (or possess).
843:Swadhritā:	Self-Carrier.
844:Swasya:	Of Beautiful Visage.
845:Pragvansha:	The Origin of all families.
846:Vanshavardhan:	He who Augments Families.
847:Bhārbhritā:	The Carrier of (the Earth's) load.
848: Kathīlā:	Repeatedly described (by the scriptures).
849: Yogi:	Ever in communion (with his world).
850:Yogesha:	Lord of all yogis.
851:Sarvākāmad:	Fulfiller of all desires.
852:Aashramah:	The Resting place for all.
853:Shraman:	The Scourge of the wicked.
854:Kshāmah:	The Queller of Every Being During the Dissolution.
855:Suparnah:	In the Form of Garuda with beautiful wings.
856:Vayuvāhan:	He who Imparts wind the capacity to move.
857:Dhanurdharah:	The Bow Weilder (Shree Rām).
858:Dhanurvedah:	An Expert in Archery.
859:Dandah:	The Staff for punishment of the wicked.
860:Damayita:	The Ruler (like Yama) to keep vile forces in control.
861:Damah:	Reforming the wicked by adequate punishment.
862:Aparājitah:	Never Defeated.
863:Sarvasaha:	Having capacity to tolerate everything.
864:Niyantā:	He who Defines every being's duty.
865:Aniyam:	Unbound by any regulation.
866:Ayamah:	Beyond the limti to Death or any bondage.

867: Satvavāna:	Having all puissance.
868: Sattvik:	Of Noble Demeanour.
869: Satya:	The Truth.
870: Satyadharmap: ārāyanah	He who Adheres to the Righteous path, the Dharma, truthfully.
871: Abhiprāyah:	The Ultimate Meaning.
872: Priyārha:	He who Deserves to be offered one's dearest object or thing.
873: Priyakrita	He Who Does What is Good (for his devotees).
874: Arhah:	Supremely Adorable for all.
875: Preetivardhan:	He who Enriches affection for Him in His Dearest votaries.
876: Vihāyasagatih:	He who Moves in the Skies.
877: Jyotih:	The Supreme Radiance.
878: Suruchih:	Having comely grace and choicest taste.
879: Hitabhuk:	He who Accepts the Offerings made in a sacrifice.
880: Vibhuh:	All Pervading.
881: Ravi:	The Usurper of All Sap of the Creation, the Sun.
882: Virochan:	He Who Spreads Light in All Directions.
883: Surya:	He who unveils the pulchritude; the Sun.
884: Savitā:	The Begetter of the Entire universe.
885: Ravilochana:	He who has the Sun as His eye.
886: Anantah:	He who is Endless.
887: Hutabhuk:	The Consumer of All offerings.
888: Bhokta:	The Enjoyer of All Natural Bounties.
889: Sukhadah:	The Bestower of Happiness (to his devotee).
890: Narkajah:	Having Infinite Births for the protection of the noble and Dharma.
891: Agrajah:	The First Born; The Primal Being.
892: Anirvannah:	He who is Never Bored (by any activity).
893: Sadāmarshee:	He who Ever Forgives the noble.
894: Lokadhishthanam:	The Prop of the Entire Realms.

895:Adbhutah:	Amazing.
896:Sanāt:	The Form At the Final Hour.
897:Sanātantamah:	The Cause and Root of All; the Oldest Being.
898:Kapilah:	The sage Kapil.
899: Kepih:	The Sun-god.
900:Apyaha	The point of Final coalescence.
901:Swastidah::	He who Ensures Welfare of All.
902:Swastikritah:	The Auspicious Refuge of the noblce.
903:Swasti:	The Embodiment of All that is Auspicious.
904:Swastibhuk:	He who protects welfare of His devotees.
905:Swastidakshinah:	The Right Hand Ensuring Welfare to His devotees.
906:Araudra:	The Embodiment of peace sans all wrath.
907:Kundali:	The wearer of the (corcodile shaped) Ear-rings as bright as the sun.
908:Chakri:	The Weilder of the Discus Sudarshan.
909:Vikrami:	He who Sits In Revolution.
910:Uoorjitashāsan:	Whose Adminstration, as Ordained through the Scriptures, is the Best.
911:Shabdātigah:	He who is Beyond the range of Voice or Sound.
912:Shabdasah:	He whose glory is Described by the Scriptures.
913:Shishirah:	The Cool Image for those afflicted by the Oppressive heat of three kinds (the physical, the mental and the spiritual).
914:Sharvarikarah:	He who is Night of Enlightenment for the learned and Night of Ignorance for the ignorants -i.e. He who Creates both sorts of Night Himself.
915:Akroora:	He who has no feeling of Cruelty.
916:Peshalah:	Supremely Beautiful Owing to his auspicious voice, mind and deeds.

917: Dakshah:	The Expert or Efficient (in every art).
918: Dakshinah:	The Destroyer.
919: Kshaminam Varah:	Best Among those who Forgives.
920: Vidwattamah:	The Most Learned Scholar.
921: Veetabhayah:	Free from all fright.
922: Punyashravan keertan:	He listening to whose glories and singing whose hymns grant all merit.
923: Uttārana:	He who takes (the soul) across the ocean of metempsychosis.
924: Dushkritaha:	He who Destroys the sin of sinner.
925: Punya:	Whose very remembrance gives one merit.
926: Duhawapnanāshan:	The Destroyer of the Nightmares.
927: Veerahā:	He who gallantly alters the course of His devotees'Destiny.
928: Rakshanah:	He who protects the noble by all means.
929: Sant:	He who spreads educatio and humility by his action and voice.
930: Jeevanah:	The Very life of all Existence.
931: Paryavastihah:	He who pervades All world But Himself Remains Stationary.
932: Anataroop:	He who Has Infinite Forms.
933: Anantashree:	He Who Has Immense Psychic powers.
934: Jitamanyu:	He who has subdued anger.
935: Bhayāpah:	He who Removes fear from His devotees'heart.
936: Chatturashtrah:	The Embodiment of all Vedic Knowledge and Just.
937: Gabheerātma:	He who has depth in His character.
938: Vidishah:	He who gives each what is due on the basis of the deed performed.
939: Vyādishah:	He who Gives Appropriate orders to all (or who Assigns every Being's Duty).
940: Dishah:	Like the Vedas showing the right directions.
941: Anādi:	He who had no Beginning.

942:Bhoorbhuvah:	The Support of this Earth.
943:Lakshmi:	The Sheen of all beauteous objects.
944:Suveerah:	He who Inspires faith in the devotees' hearts.
945:Ruchirāngadah:	He who Dons auspicious armlets.
946:Jananah:	The Origin of All Beings.
947:Janmajanmādi:	The Root Cause of all beings' birth.
948:Bheemah:	Terrible for the wicked.
949:Bheema-parākramah:	performer of the Terrifying feats for the wicked.
950:Ādharnilaya:	The Support of the Earth and all the beings.
951:Adhāta:	He who could not be carried (created) by anyone.
952:Pushpahās:	He whose laughter is like the Blooming flower.
953:Prajāgarah:	He who is ever conscious and Awakened.
954:Uoordhvagah:	He who Dwells at the top.
955:Satpathāchar:	He who Ever Moves on the Righteous Path.
956:Prānadah:	He who Resuscitates the dead (like Pareekshitah, who was born dead, but brought to life by Lord Krishna, an Incarnation of Lord Vishnu).
957:Pranavah:	The Form of the syllable Onkar.
958:Panah:	He Whose Behaviour Is Ideal with all; Worldliwise.
959:Pramānam:	The Evidence (or Self Evident).
960:Pranānilaya:	The Basis of life.
961:Prānabrita:	The Nourisher of life.
962:Prānjeevan:	The Vital Air to keep all beings alive.
963:Tattvam:	The Essence (or the Reality).
964:Tattvavita:	He who knows the Reality.
965:Ekātma:	Unique; without A Second.
966:Janmamrityu-jarātigah:	Beyond life and death or decay or beyone mortal bondage.
967:Bhoorbhuvahs Wastaruh:	The Tree of Existence permeating all the three Realms.

968:Tarah:	He who makes one (his devotee) transcend the sea of life and death.
969:Savita:	The Grand Deity causing birth of every being; the Sun.
970:Prapitāmah:	The Sire of the Grand Deity Brahma.
971:Yagyah:	The cause of all activities the world.
972:Yagyapatih:	The Lord of all yagyas or the Decider of all activities.
973:Yajwa:	He who is also the Host of the yagya or sacrifice.
974:Yagyangah:	The Embodiment of all organs of a yagya or the One who decides every activity in a yagya.
975:Yagyavāhan:	The Moving Spirit behind every yagya-the prime Mover of every activity.
976:Yagyabhrit:	He Who Nourishes every activity.
977:Yagyakrita:	The performer of the yagya or who makes every yagya an accomplish-ment.
978:Yagyee:	The Ultimate goal of every yagya or the final outcome of every or the final outcome of every activity.
979:Yagyabhuk:	He who Enjoys the outcome of every activity.
980:Yagyasādhana:	The Deity or the Ultimate Aim for which the Yagyas are performed.
981:Yagyantakrita:	He who Ends every yagya or who Bestows the Reward of every yagya.
982:Yagyaguhyam:	The Imperceptible Manifestation of Knowledge through Yagya.
983:Annam:	The Bestower of Cereal or Food for every Being.
984:Annād:	The Eater of all food.
985:Atmayoni:	He who caused His own creation;or the Self-created.
986:Swayamjātah:	He who creates Himself at His will.

987: Vaikhānah:	The Digger of Earth (Lord Vishnu dug earth in His Boar Incarnation to slay Hiranyakashapa who dwelled inside the bowels of the earth).
988: Sāmgayanah:	He who Chants the Hymns of Sām Veda.
989: Devakinandan:	Son of Mother Devaki (in His Shree Krishna Incarnation).
990: Srishtā:	The procreator of All Realms; the Cause of Existnece.
991: Kshiteesha:	Master of Earth.
992: Papanāshan:	The Destroyer of Sin (merely by His remembrance and worship).
993: Shankhabhrita:	The Weilder of the conch-shell called Panchajanya.
994: Nandaki:	The Weilder of the Sword called Nandak.
995: Chakri:	The Weilder of the Discus called Sudarshan.
996: Sharngadhanva:	The Weilder of the Bow called Sharnga.
997: Gadādhar:	The Weilder of the mace called Kaumudi.
998: Rathāngpāni:	He who weilded the wheel of the chariot as his discus to challenge Bheeshma Pitamah in the Mahabharat war.
999: Askshobhya:	He who can't be frightened by anyone or anything.
1000: Sarvapraharan: āyudhah	He who is the Weilder of all those Known and nuknown weapons used in war.

Om Namo Bhagwate Vasudevaaya